FOR BRUCE, TODD, AND TENLEY,

incomparable each

VOLUME II

Sight and Sound

A Manual of Aural Musicianship

LEO KRETER

*California State University
Fullerton, California*

PRENTICE-HALL, INC., Englewood Cliffs, New Jersey

Library of Congress Cataloging in Publication Data

KRETER, LEO, date
    Sight and sound: a manual of aural musicianship.

    1. Ear training.   I. Title.
MT35.K825S5   780'.77   75-1375
ISBN 0-13-809913-8 (v. 2)

© 1976 by PRENTICE-HALL, INC.
Englewood Cliffs, New Jersey

Printed in the United States of America

10   9   8   7   6   5   4   3   2   1

PRENTICE-HALL INTERNATIONAL, INC., London
PRENTICE-HALL OF AUSTRALIA, PTY. LTD., Sydney
PRENTICE-HALL OF CANADA, LTD., Toronto
PRENTICE-HALL OF INDIA PRIVATE LIMITED, New Delhi
PRENTICE-HALL OF JAPAN, INC., Tokyo
PRENTICE-HALL OF SOUTHEAST ASIA (PTE.) LTD., Singapore

Contents

v

Preface

Students who choose to become music majors in college are usually experienced performers but are largely ignorant of theoretical matters, and, except for a fortunate few, usually have had no prior instruction in a systematic study of the aural forces which interrelate to produce the music they perform so well. In particular, they experience difficulty in correlating sound with symbol and in translating the sounds they hear into musical notation, and are often discouraged by their initial attempts to improve their aural awareness, recognizing the gap that exists between their performance skills and their capacity to identify the organic relationships within the music they are studying. Accordingly, these two volumes are addressed to the serious music student who wishes to improve his aural skills.

These companion volumes cover the *diatonic* aspects of aural musicianship, though necessarily they delve into chromaticism to a limited extent. They constitute a study of those basic aural factors most capable of identification and systematic consideration, with constant focus on the structural relationships which underlie triadic music. They are intended as supporting volumes to a general theory text, and therefore some knowledge of the basic musical elements is assumed, though certain concepts are presented in moderate detail insofar as they relate specifically to a particular aural problem under study.

Exercises of many types form the core of the text. Many of these are taken from standard music literature, while other exercises are devised especially to point up certain aural problems and to provide concentrated practice in dealing with them. Examples taken from literature are usually incomplete segments, since the passages chosen illustrate specific problems which may not be inherent in the remainder of the composition. C clefs are not used, and no transposing instrumental lines occur. Only the standard treble and bass clefs are to be found, since the handling of other clefs is a special notational problem not directly related to the aims of this book.

Rhythm, melody, counterpoint, and harmony are treated in approximately equal proportions in a cumulative progression from the most fundamental to the complex, and the interaction among these elements is increasingly stressed through the course of the text. Complexity is regarded as an elaboration or variant of a fundamental underlying structure, and the primary emphasis in the text is for the listener to discover that fundamental underlying structure, whatever the degree of elaboration and complication that envelops it.

Traditionally, ear training has been regarded as the transcribing of musical lines through dictation. A substantial amount of dictation does occur in the text as one means of strengthening the ties between actual sound and printed notation, but equal emphasis is placed on other factors in listening, and the listener is asked to respond in many different ways other than to notate sounds —to identify, to select, to correct, and to describe what he hears.

There are many techniques to improve aural acuity, and any approach that brings results should be encouraged; conversely any approach that produces only frustration without perceptible progress should be abandoned. Nothing, however, is as beneficial as the immediate feedback from another sympathetic musician who is anxious to help and to be helped in turn. Above all, nothing can replace the sympathetic, perceptive, and experienced teacher, particularly if he himself has faced the same kinds of struggles and frustrations his students face. Flexibility is the most essential factor in ear training, and any technique that works is valid, however it may differ from standard techniques or from techniques suggested in this text. Accordingly, this text should be regarded as a guidebook rather than a prescriptive manual, indicating a broad path toward a commonly desired goal.

My students are largely responsible for this book. Their needs provided the stimulus for beginning, and their continuing desire to improve as musicians has brought many teaching rewards during the course of the book's development. If, having used the book, students are better able to perceive the interrelationship of the various musical elements operating in an unfamiliar piece of music, that sensitivity will make their musical lives far richer, and their love of music far deeper, than ever before, and they will thereafter communicate this depth of understanding as they discuss and perform all music literature.

On Using This Text

The two volumes into which this text is divided contain twenty-four chapters, unequally apportioned. Volume I contains fourteen chapters and Volume II contains ten, the final two of which are a comprehensive review of all the material in both volumes. Since the progression is cumulative throughout both volumes, the earlier chapters treat relatively basic concepts and can therefore be covered faster than the later chapters in Volume II, which involve a synthesis of concepts and techniques.

Every student is unique and every class situation is different, and the author assumes that these volumes will be used differently in different contexts. However, since only the diatonic aspects of aural musicianship are considered, in most institutions this text would be appropriate for the first-year theory courses, with some overlap probable with the beginning of the second year. As a student, you should begin assignments in the first volume immediately at the start of the course, and the text should be used regularly throughout the term. Depending upon your previous experience, you may find it desirable to study the first six chapters in pairs, rather than singly. In many instances, Volume I may not be completed by the mid-year point, but it is possible to complete both volumes within a full year, assuming that you practice consistently.

In each chapter the exercises are divided into two general categories—Performing and Listening—under each of which several different kinds of exercises may occur. It is possible and often useful to interchange the exercises, using Performing exercises for Listening, and the reverse. An abundance of exercises has been provided to give ample opportunity for practice, more than you may find necessary, but you should practice only as many as *you* need to practice in any given problem area. If a problem is encountered in a particular chapter, go back to an appropriate earlier chapter and review the groundwork which underlies your present difficulty. Continually assess your strengths and weaknesses, and resist the understandable temptation to spend more time with the former than with the latter. From the simplest to the most complex chapters, you are strongly urged to invent your own exercises, using the exercises in the text as a guideline. Pursue other paths and different composers, modifying the exercises and approaches in this book to your particular set of circumstances.

The exercises are designed to be challenging, often requiring a considerable degree of effort. Unless you are satisfied with slovenly performance, it is difficult to engage in the exercises in an unthinking, mechanical manner. It is essential that you approach each exercise with a constant awareness of the precise inflection of every pitch, that you know key signatures well, and that you thoroughly understand the theoretical basis governing interval sizes. You may practice certain of the exercises profitably by yourself, but many require at least one other person, and, in general, the most benefit will accrue if you choose a partner or form a small group and practice together on a regularly scheduled basis. A written schedule of group practice times should be established at the beginning of the course and should be adhered to throughout the course. As with all skills that require practice, more is to be gained from frequent brief sessions than from occasional intensive sessions, and habitual daily practice will produce the most successful results.

The Appendix at the end of each volume contains the information needed to execute the Listening assignments in each chapter. You will consult it continually as you perform the various exercises, and you should always check your dictation with it immediately upon completion of the dictation exercises. Recordings of all the Listening assignments are available from the publisher, and they are useful in a listening laboratory situation when a partner is not available, but they should not be regarded as a wholly satisfactory substitute for a sympathetic and helpful partner who can perform the exercises according to *your* needs.

As with all personal things, only *you* can learn for yourself. You will have strengths and weaknesses in ear training, as in all disciplines. Avoid the human temptation to ignore your weaknesses and concentrate on your strengths. Accept the fact that you are imperfect, and then strive to improve. You can always be a better musician, and as your musicianship improves, your strengths become increasingly valuable.

XV

Basic Chord Progressions
Primary Triads Only
The Dominant Seventh Chord

In previous chapters dealing with harmony, emphasis was placed on identification of individual chord types, either separately or in short progressions. In this chapter, emphasis will be placed on the recognition of changing chord roots in chord progressions. Chord choice will be limited to the three primary triads (tonic, subdominant, and dominant—sometimes also called "principal triads"), which are the principal structural chords used in any given key and which are also the most frequently used chords in the key.

In major keys, the three primary triads are all major chords; in minor keys the tonic and subdominant are minor chords, while the dominant is most often a major chord (a major dominant chord contains the important leading tone tendency, while a minor dominant chord contains the more neutral subtonic seventh degree, and hence exhibits far less tendency to resolve to the tonic). Since the root of the tonic is the first scale degree, the root of the subdominant the fourth scale degree, and the root of the dominant the fifth, the chords are customarily referred to as the I, IV, and V chords respectively, and are indicated by a Roman numeral corresponding to the root. Major chords will always be indicated in this text by large Roman numerals, while minor chords will be indicated by small Roman numerals without the cross bars. Thus, in minor keys, the tonic and subdominant triads are indicated by i and iv respectively, while the dominant, because it is a major chord, is indicated by V. Refinements to this chord symbol system will occur in subsequent chapters as the occasion demands.

The most important single chord progression in all tonal music is the

1

progression V–I (or I–V). Continual alternation between tonic and dominant chords is the basis for many, if not most, simple songs (with occasional, and usually brief, excursions to other chords—often the subdominant).

In any given key, the tonic and dominant triads will share a *common tone*—a pitch class which appears in both chords.

FIGURE 1

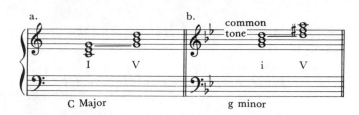

Customarily, in connecting two chords with common tones, composers either sustained or repeated the common tone in the same voice, thus ensuring the smoothest possible linear flow. They naturally did not hold the common tone when it did not suit their purposes (when dissimilarity between chords was to be emphasized). In general, the common tone was held more consistently in choral (or vocal) music than in instrumental music, particularly for the piano solo. Whether held or not, the common tone is always present (theoretically) in the tonic–dominant relationship (and in the tonic–subdominant relationship as well). For the present, the common tone will be held more often than not, which should be regarded as the norm.

FIGURE 2

Note that when the common tone is held, the other voices move as little as possible (by stepwise motion preferably), which is also the smoothest possible connection. Also note that they *may* occupy a unison together, and often do (tenor and bass, Figure 2–b, third chord).

The progression tonic-subdominant-tonic is handled similarly, with a common tone and stepwise motion.

FIGURE 3

Sing the following progressions. They may also be played, but they *must* be sung. Everyone should sing the bass line first, which consists of chord roots only, before dividing into parts. Observe the difference between I–V and I–IV. In the former progression, the bass rises by a fifth while in the latter it moves by only a fourth. The dominant is a slightly more "distant" progression than the subdominant, and the subdominant sounds slightly "heavier." Because of its leading tone tendency, the progression V–I sounds stronger than the progression IV–I, perhaps because it seems more "different" from the tonic than does the subdominant chord. These are decidedly subjective descriptions of both chord progressions, and each person will hear these progressions in his uniquely personal way, which may differ markedly from the description given above. This is fine and desirable, so long as each person not only notes that the progressions *are* different, but that they possess unique qualities which differentiate them one from the other, and that he learns to listen for these qualities in the progressions. The presence of the leading tone in the V chord is equally as indicative of "dominant quality" as the root relationship with the tonic.

Practice the progressions below in a variety of keys other than those given. Sing on a neutral vowel, or sing the number of the chord root as you change chords (I–V–I). *Everyone*—not only the basses—should be aware when a chord changes. Listen closely for the leading tone—tonic melodic motion.

1.

Major

2.

minor

i   V   i   i   V   i   i   V   i

3.

Major

I   IV   I   I   IV   I   I   IV   I

4.

minor

i   iv   i   i   iv   i   i   iv   i

5.

Allegro moderato

I ————————— IV ————————— I ——————————
(also in minor)

6.

I ————————— IV ————————— I ——————————
(also in minor)

7.

i —————— V ———— i ——————
(also in Major)

8.

i ———— V ———— i ———— V ———— i ————
(also in Major)

Chords IV and V in any given key do *not* share a common tone; hence all the pitch classes of the V chord will be different from those of the IV chord (Figure 4, a and b). In such a progression, the upper voices customarily move in contrary motion to the direction of the bass voice. Note that the root moves by step rather than by skip as in the previous progressions (Fig. 4, c and d).

FIGURE 4

The reverse of this progression (V–IV) is less frequently encountered, being regarded by most composers and theoreticians as a retrogression that lacks propulsive energy. The following exercises explore various aspects of the subdominant-dominant progression. Sing (or play) as before.

9.

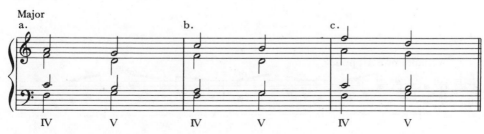

10.

minor

11.

12.

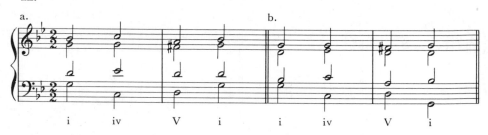

13.

14.

15.

16.

THE V⁷ CHORD

Frequently the V⁷ (dominant seventh) is substituted for the simple dominant triad (V). The V⁷ consists of four different pitch classes, the last of which forms a dissonant minor seventh interval with the root, which requires resolution in the following chord. The dominant seventh chord can always be recognized by its distinctive aural quality—a major triad with a minor seventh. The basic melodic tendency of all sevenths is to descend by step to a tone in the following chord, and the V⁷ chord follows this standard resolution.

FIGURE 5

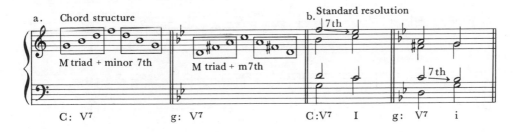

Note that the standard resolution produces a tonic triad with three roots and a third, but no fifth. When the leading tone of the V⁷ is in an inner voice (alto or tenor), that voice may skip down rather than move up according to its natural tendency, producing a complete tonic triad with the root doubled.

FIGURE 6

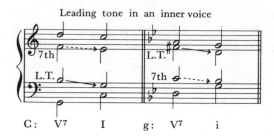

Leading tone in an inner voice

C:　V⁷　　I　　　g:　V⁷　　i

The following exercises explore various aspects of the V⁷ chord and its resolution. Note particularly the resolution of the chord seventh and the leading tone.

PERFORMING

17.

Allegro non troppo

V⁷ ———————————————————————————— I

18.

Allegro

F:　V⁷ ———————————— V⁷ ———————————— I

B♭:　V⁷ ———————————— V⁷ ———————————— I

E♭:　V ———————————— V⁷ ———————————— I　　A♭:V ———— etc.

Treat each *root* of the final tonic as the root of a dominant seventh in a new key a fifth down (or a fourth above).

19.

20

21.

CHORD CONNECTION

Strict adherence to the principles of voice leading considered thus far produces smooth and logical musical flow which also, paradoxically, tends to be dull and predictable. In longer progressions, composers often enhanced the sense of forward motion by changing chords at important structural points (points of greatest anticipation) and by freely moving the voices (especially the soprano) when a given chord is repeated. The listener may well expect that when a given chord is reiterated, the soprano will be active, often outlining the triad, and that in general harmonic changes will reinforce the meter, with most important chord changes occurring over the bar lines.

The tonic should be heard as the stable "home" chord, the dominant as the "away" chord, the one most different from the tonic, with a strong tendency to return to the tonic. Certain substantial passages consist solely of movement from I to V, with a subsequent return to I.

The subdominant often precedes the dominant. It may be regarded in that context as a pre-dominant chord, moving to the dominant by stepwise movement. Sometimes the subdominant returns to the tonic in a rather neutral progression (less decisive than I-V) without moving on to the dominant. It is somewhat less important than the tonic and dominant chords in most contexts.

22.

23.

Linear Chord Connection

The bass line determines each chord position in any progression, and it is therefore essential to keep the movement of the bass in mind at all times as you listen harmonically.

Practice the following simple chord progressions, outlining each specified chord up and down from the bass note, maintaining particular awareness of the movement of the bass at each chord change. The meter should be changed as needed to adjust to the particular situation.

FIGURE 7

Specified
progression: I   I⁶   IV   IV⁶   V⁷   I

24. A: I   IV   I⁶   V   I
25. B♭: I   V   I⁶   IV   IV⁶   V⁷   I
26. A♭: I   I⁶   IV   V   IV⁶   V   V⁶   I
27. G: I   V⁶   I   IV   I⁶   V   IV⁶   V⁷   I
28. a: i   iv   iv⁶   V   i
29. b♭: i   i⁶   iv   iv⁶   V   V⁶   i
30. c: i   V⁶   i   iv   iv⁶   V   i⁶   iv   V   i
31. g: i   i⁶   V   iv⁶   iv   i⁶   V⁷   i
32. Improvise similar progressions using the same procedures. Most progressions will be easiest to negotiate in a comfortable (low) key. Red calls out chord numerals as blue outlines the chords; end eventually on a a V–I cadence progression and reverse roles. This provides excellent practice is visualizing chords in notation.

LISTENING

In Chapter XII you were expected to distinguish between chords in root position and inversions. Remember that, in outlining a triad from the bass up, if the two bottom intervals are thirds, the chord is in root position (1–3–5–3–1); if the third is in the bass, and the upper interval is a fourth, the chord is in first inversion (3–5–8–5–3); and if the fifth is in the bass, and the lower interval is a fourth, the chord is in second inversion (5–8–3–8–5). First inversion chords sound somewhat lighter in weight (to most people) than root position chords, and, being less forceful, are often found on the unaccented beats, while root position chords are more often found on the accented beats. First inversion chords are useful for a variety of purposes, of which three are particularly important: 1) as relief from the aural monotony of root movement, 2) as connecting chords, filling in a gap of a fourth or fifth, and 3) as a means of avoiding parallel fifths or octaves between the bass and some other voice.

Determining Chord Roots—
Root Position and First Inversion

(Appendix, p. 215)

Most of the chords in the following exercises will be in root position, but some will be heard in first inversion. In both instances, the root remains the same—only the bass is different. In the following series of chord progressions, you are to sing the *root*, not (necessarily) the bass, as each chord is played. Sustain the *root* until a new chord with a different root is played. On subsequent hearings, note which chords are in first inversion (bass note different from the root you are singing) and listen to the distinctive quality of the first inversion. If possible, write the chord numerals below the line. Be specific about first inversions (I⁶, V⁶, etc.). Initially it may be helpful to sing the tonic, subdominant, and dominant notes before beginning each exercise.

FIGURE 8

33.

Moderato

34.

Moderato

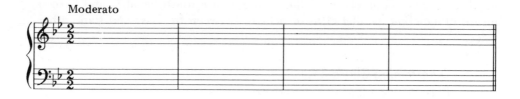

35.

Moderato

36.

Reduced from Bach

37.

Clementi

38.

Recognition of a Specific Progression

(Appendix, p. 217)

39– In the next series, you are to raise your hand when you hear the chord
42. progression specified. As soon as the final chord of the progression
is played, lower your hand again. The key, tempo, and meter will *not*
be established before each exercise, unless specific instructions are given
to the contrary; you must infer these factors from the context. As always,
invent others for further practice.

Two-Voice Dictation

(Appendix, p. 218)

Listen to each of the following excerpts completely before writing. Note
the chordal implications of this two-voice counterpoint, and write the appropriate Roman numerals under each chord. Then write the soprano and

bass lines. The tonal center will be established before each exercise, but not necessarily the tempo or the meter. These must be inferred completely from the musical context itself.

If possible, two different instruments should be used for the dictation.

43.   44.

45.

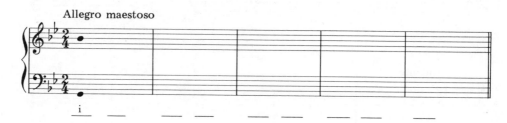

46.

47.

Clementi, Op.36, No.2, II

Andantino

Four-Voice Dictation

(Appendix, p. 220)

A series of short progressions will be played. On the first hearing, write the chord numeral below the bass clef. On subsequent hearings, notate the bass and soprano voices. These are the most important voices; if this dictation comes easily, listen carefully and notate the alto and tenor voices as well. The tempi will be mostly moderate to slow, and the tonality will be established before each set of exercises in a common key. In a few exercises, the initial bass and soprano pitches will be given; for these exercises, the tonality will *not* be established beforehand.

48.

49.

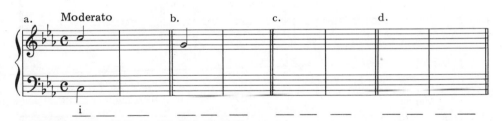

50.

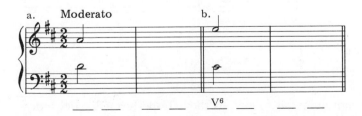

51.

52.

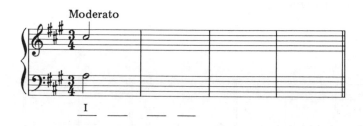

53.

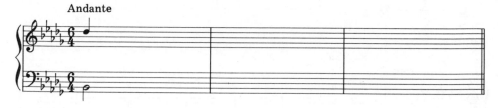

54.

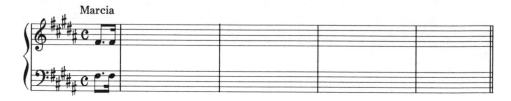

Error Detection

(Appendix, p. 222)

Several series of Roman numerals follow. As they are performed, each series will be played incorrectly. At first there will be no rhythm pattern (only block chords), and relatively few errors will occur. As the texture and rhythm become more complex, the errors increase. Raise your hand when you hear an error; if possible, correct it. Identification, however, is more important than correction at this stage.

55. A: I   V   I   IV   I
56. B: I   IV   V   I   I⁶   V   I
57. b: i   iv   V   iv⁶   V   V⁷   i
58. D ¾ :   I   IV | I   IV   V | IV⁶   V⁷ | I ||
59. E♭ 4/4 :   I   I⁶   IV | V⁷   I⁶   I | IV   IV⁶   V   V⁶ | I   V   I ||
60. e ⅜ :   i   i⁶   iv | V | i⁶   iv⁶   V | iv   iv⁶ | V   V⁷   i ||

Error Detection from Score

(Appendix, p. 223)

The following exercises from literature are notated correctly, but will be played incorrectly. On the first hearing, place a check mark over each error you observe. On subsequent hearings, identify the errors, notating them directly on the printed score. Errors will occur in chord type, chord position, or chord function (the Roman numeral indicating the root).

61.

Schumann, *Freue Dich, O Meine Seele*

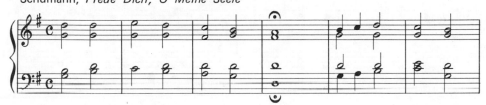

62.

Crüger, *Herr ich hade missgehandelt*

63.

Chopin, Mazurka (Op. Post.)

64.

Grieg, *Ase's Death*

Error Detection by Memory

(Appendix, p. 226)

The next exercises are unlike any previously encountered. You are to carefully examine each exercise for a brief period, memorize it, then determine whether or not the version played back is correct. Raise your hand to stop the music whenever an error occurs. After the excerpt has been played once you may reexamine the score; all subsequent playings will follow this second examination of the score. If possible, correct the errors on subsequent hearings, but recognition of an error is more important than correction by memory at this point. Errors may occur in chord type, chord position, or chord function. Rhythm and melody are not concerns in these exercises.

65.

66.

67.

68.

69.

70.

XVI

Rhythmic Counterpoint—Review; More Two-Voice Counterpoint; Similar Registers, Rests, Dissonant Intervals

RHYTHMIC COUNTERPOINT (REVIEW)

Complex rhythms, such as are more commonly found in instrumental music than in vocal music, have not been recently encountered in this text. These initial exercises are intended as a review and extension of instrumental rhythmic contexts; all require at least two participants, and preferably three. The exercises should be performed on two different vowels and two different pitches, or on two instruments on different pitches. Both performers may read the complete score, but preferably each should cover the other's part, reading only his own, as if performing chamber music. A third participant is needed, of course, for the exercises in three-part counterpoint, but the third participant could profitably conduct the two-voice drills, correcting errors as they occur. Always exchange parts after performing each exercise.

PERFORMING

Two-Voice Counterpoint

1.

Allegro non troppo

2.

7.

Allegretto

8.

Grazioso

9.

Allegro moderato

10.

LISTENING

Two-Voice Rhythmic Dictation

(Appendix, p. 229)

Listen to each exercise completely; then notate both parts, one on the top, and one on the bottom space of the staff provided. The parts will be played at two different pitch levels; initially the tempo will be established before each exercise, but this may be dropped in the later exercises. Three hearings should be sufficient. In several of the exercises in this chapter, a structural *motive* is used significantly. This is a short rhythmic-melodic pattern that is repeated or varied.

11.

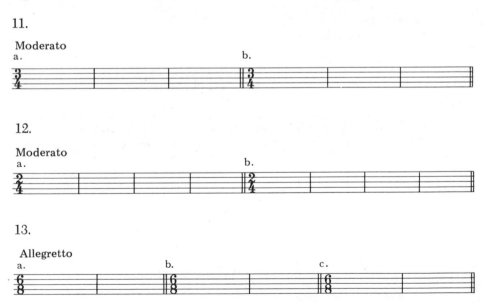

14.

Andante

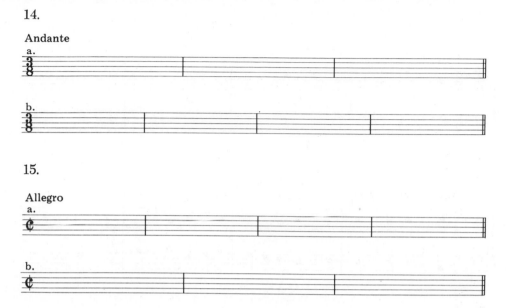

15.

Allegro

MORE COMPLEX TWO-VOICE COUNTERPOINT

While the exercises in Chapter XIII consisted of continuous melodic activity in both soprano and bass voices, in this chapter occasional rests are included in the texture, and the two voices will sometimes be heard in the same register. In general, the exercises are more challenging than those encountered previously, for they are extended to include more dissonant intervals at structurally important places (tritone, diminished seventh, minor seventh, perfect fourth).

In Exercises 16–21, the dissonant intervals of the seventh, tritone, and fourth are stressed and their resolutions are indicated by arrows. Sevenths resolve down (normally), and the tritone normally resolves according to its spelling (augmented fourth resolves outward, diminished fifth resolves inward). Listen for the dissonance and the resolution as you sing or play the exercises.

PERFORMING

16.

Moderato

17.

18.

19.

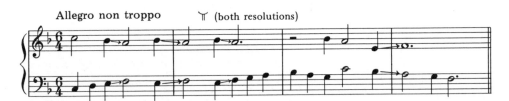

20.

21.

LISTENING

The exercises that follow are of three types: 1) dictation with notated sign-posts, 2) straight dictation, without signposts, and 3) error detection in excerpts from musical literature.

In the first two categories, the initial exercises will focus on voices in a similar register; later exercises will be between soprano and bass voices.

Dictation with Notated Signposts

(Appendix, p. 230)

Write the following exercises after they have been played (or sung). Listen for important intervals at structurally significant places, for rests, for tendency tones, for complementary rhythms, and for resolution of sevenths and tritones such as you have recently practiced. Try not to listen to each line separately, but rather to their interrelationships. Rhythmic-melodic motives will be heard in certain passages. Recognition of their occurrence will help break up the passages into shorter, more easily digestible units.

22.

23.

24.

25.

26.

Bach, Chorale No.81

(Andante)

27.

Allegro

28.

Tchaikovsky, Symphony No.6, IV

Andante (molto)

29.

Allegro

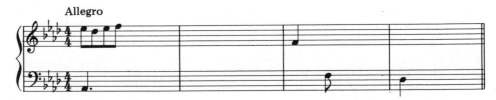

30.

Allegro moderato

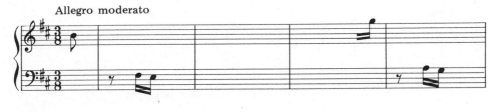

31.

Allegro non troppo

Dictation without Notated Signposts

(*Appendix, p. 233*)

The initial pitch or pitches, but not necessarily the initial rhythmic values, are given for each of the following exercises. Listen to the complete excerpt before beginning to write. Establishment of tempo and key will depend upon circumstances; whenever possible, this practice should be avoided. Structural motives will appear less frequently than with earlier exercises, since the melodic content is generally simpler.

32.

Moderato

33.

34.

35.

36.

37.

Franck, Prelude, Chorale and Fugue

38.

39.

Bach, Chorale No.68

(Andante)

40.

Flowing

41.

Mendelssohn, *Hope,* Op.38, No.4

Andante

42.

Haydn, *The Creation,* No.2

Allegro moderato

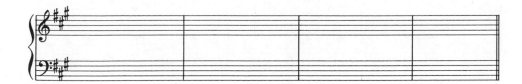

Error Detection

(Appendix, p. 235)

The following excerpts, printed correctly below, will be performed with errors. Make a check mark over each point where an error occurs and (later) notate each error directly on the printed score. A colored pencil is useful for this purpose. Instead of notating the errors, it may be preferable to stop the music when an error occurs, correcting it orally. Errors will be melodic or rhythmic, or may occur in a series or individually. Listen for the larger series errors first, concentrating on single errors later. Neither tempo nor key will be established before the exercises.

43.

Mendelssohn, *Folk Song,* Op.53, No.5

44.

Adapted from Brahms, *Romance,* Op.118, No.5

45.

Bach, Chorale No.107

46.

Haydn, *The Creation,* No.2

47.

Brahms, *Variations on a Theme of Joseph Haydn,* Var.3

48.

49.

Haydn, *The Creation,* No.29

Adagio (Andante)

50.

Haydn, *The Creation,* No.27

Vivace

51.

Chopin, *Valse Brilliante*

(Moderato)

52.

Bach, Italian Concerto, III

Allegro (Presto)

53.

Franck, Sonata for Violin and Piano, IV

Allegretto poco mosso

XVII

Cadence Patterns; Basic Chord Progression—Primary Triads (continued)

CADENCE PATTERNS

A phrase normally ends with a concluding harmonic progression that brings the musical motion to a point of rest, usually on the tonic or dominant chord; such concluding progressions are called *cadences*. Though theoretically any progression *could* end a phrase, surprisingly few such progressions are commonly used. In this chapter we will be concerned with only three cadences—the authentic and half cadences, which are by far the most common, and the plagal cadence, which is found less frequently.

All cadences involve two chords, though the more structurally significant cadences are often preceded by one or more preparatory chords which are clearly intended to be heard as part of the cadence progression. The single most important cadence—that which ends the majority of compositions, the majority of formal sections within each composition, and the majority of periods within each section—is the authentic cadence, the progression V–I. Not every V–I progression constitutes a cadence—only that which concludes a phrase and which, with the support of the melody and rhythm, brings the musical motion to a point of (relative) rest.

Any cadence is said to be "perfect" if the root of the final chord is doubled in the soprano (Figure 1a). If the third or fifth is in the soprano, the cadence is regarded as "imperfect" (Figure 1b–c). A perfect authentic cadence is the strongest possible concluding progression, involving the most basic progression in music (V–I), the resolution of the leading tone, and the doubling of the root, which is the tonic of the key.

FIGURE 1

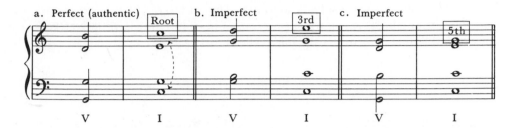

The half cadence comes to rest on V, which may be preceded by any chord (frequently I or IV). It often occurs as a preliminary cadence ending the first phrase of a period, with the more final authentic cadence ending the concluding phrase of the period. Most periods consist of two phrases—*antecedent* and *consequent*—the second of which completes the musical idea begun in the first, bringing the period to a complete harmonic close.

FIGURE 2

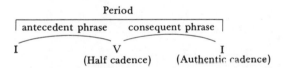

The plagal cadence (IV–I) is more rarely encountered, usually to be found at the end of a piece (Handel, particularly, was fond of this progression) and most often as a postscript to the piece, following a more conventional authentic cadence. The "Amen" frequently sung after the final verse of a hymn is an example of such a postscript. In such a context, the plagal cadence conveys a "weighty" effect; should one occur at the end of a phrase (usually antecedent) within a composition, it seems less "weighty" and less conclusive than an authentic cadence (which often follows).

Throughout this chapter, note the cadences and their relative effects in different contexts.

CHORD PATTERNS

Composers have commonly employed several basic chord patterns in developing their musical ideas—patterns that are heard as a unit. Once the pattern begins, the outcome is readily predictable. Several of these progressions were encountered in Chapter XV but were not specifically identified as recurrent patterns. To these is added a new, easily recognized cadential pattern—the cadential $^6_4$. In this pattern a tonic $^6_4$ chord (I chord in second inversion) precedes the dominant chord in an authentic cadence, adding strength and weight to the cadence through the dissonance of a fourth resolving to a consonant third, and a sixth resolving to a fifth. The unstable $^6_4$ chord occurs on a relatively strong beat. Perform the progression in Figure 3 in a variety of keys and with different spacings of the initial chord.

FIGURE 3

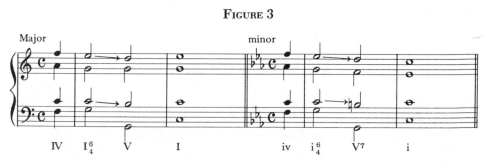

The two initial exercises emphasize the characteristic lower interval of the fourth, and the resolution of the I $^6_4$ to the V chord progressing to the tonic. Sing them in both major and minor keys.

1.

Other chord patterns are perhaps less distinctive, consisting of more commonplace chords, but they are used often enough to warrant isolating and practicing them. Sing these patterns until each takes on a personal identity in your mind's ear.

First considered are circular patterns (or neighboring chord patterns), in which the musical motion digresses from the original chord, then returns immediately to it. Next are the progressive patterns in which the motion is away from the original chord. Practice all these patterns in both major and minor keys, remembering to supply the leading tone accidental in minor keys. As you sing, pay particular attention to the bass line which determines each pattern.

Circular Patterns (Neighboring Chord)

3.

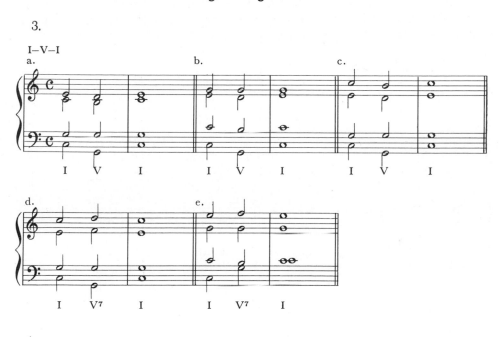

4.

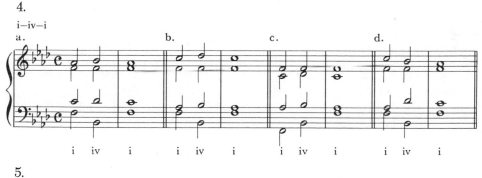

5.

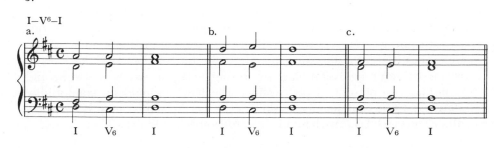

Progressive Patterns

6.

I–I⁶–IV

7.

i–iv–V–i

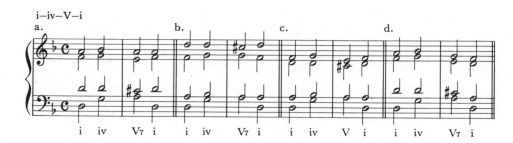

8.

I–I⁶–IV–IV⁶–V–V⁶–I

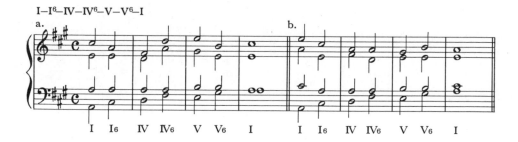

9. As a variant of the above procedure, and as a check on understanding, assign one of the patterns just studied to four people, each to take a different starting pitch (voice part). They are to be given the spacing of the initial chord and the Roman numerals of the progression. Without looking at any written progression, they are to sing, with correct voice leading and doubling, the prescribed progression. The tempo should be comfortably slow and even throughout. As skill develops, the tempo may be accelerated. The voice leading should be carefully checked by all others.

LISTENING

Soprano and Bass Factors

(*Appendix, p. 243*)

A series of unrelated chords will be played. After each is played, immediately sing the soprano note, then the bass note, and then the intervening notes, noting the quality and position of the chord, and identifying these factors. Assume augmented triads and V^7 chords to be in root position. There will be a pause before each chord.

FIGURE 4

Major—root pos.   minor—2nd inv.

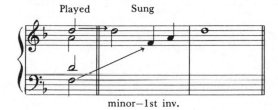

minor—1st inv.

10. 1. 2. 3. 4. 5. 6. 7. 8. 9. 10. 11. 12. 13. 14. 15. 16.

11. 1. 2. 3. 4. 5. 6. 7. 8. 9. 10. 11. 12. 13. 14. 15. 16.

PERFORMING

Linear Chord Changes

The next exercises are primarily a review of basic chord progressions expanded in linear motion. As in Chapter XV, most will be outlined from the bass up, but a few will stress outlining from the top down. The implied harmony is analyzed below the staff.

12.

13.

14.

15.

16.

V———— i ———— i⁶₄———— V———— i ————

LISTENING

Identification of a Specified Chord Progression in a Series

(Appendix, p. 244)

17– A given chord progression will be specified at the beginning of each
21. exercise. Raise your hand when you hear that progression, and lower it
after the final chord of the progression. The key, tempo, and meter will
not be established before each exercise unless prior instructions are given
to the contrary. The suggested exercises in the Appendix may be reused
with other chord progressions specified, and, as always, you are encouraged to invent other exercises for additional practice.

Determining Chord Roots—Root Position, First Inversion, Cadential ⁶₄ Progression

(Appendix, p. 246)

The following exercises are similar to those in Chapter XV, in which you are
to identify and sing the *root* (not necessarily the bass) of each chord in the
progression. Sustain the root until a new chord with a different root is played.
Though technically the root of the cadential I ⁶₄ chord is the tonic, sing the
dominant as its root, since the chord resolves immediately to dominant harmony and functions more as a dominant than a tonic chord. With additional
hearings you should be able to write the chord numerals below the line provided. Before beginning, sing the tonic, subdominant, and dominant scale
degrees as a means of orientation.

22.

Andante

23.

Mozart, Sonata, K.332, I

Allegro

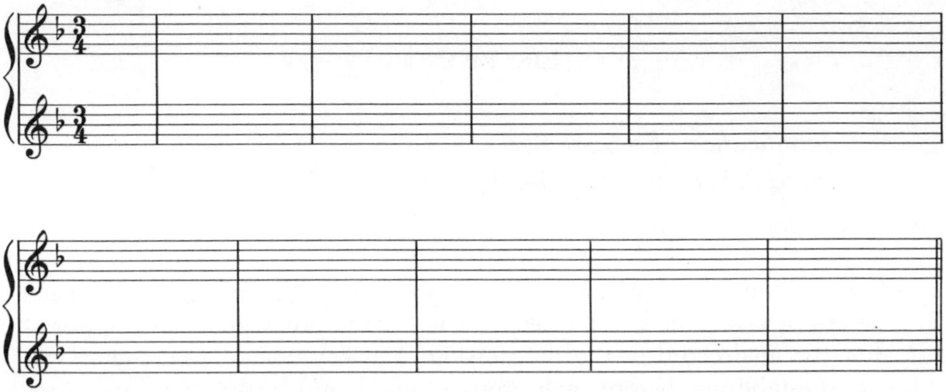

24.

Mozart, Sonata, K.280, III

Presto

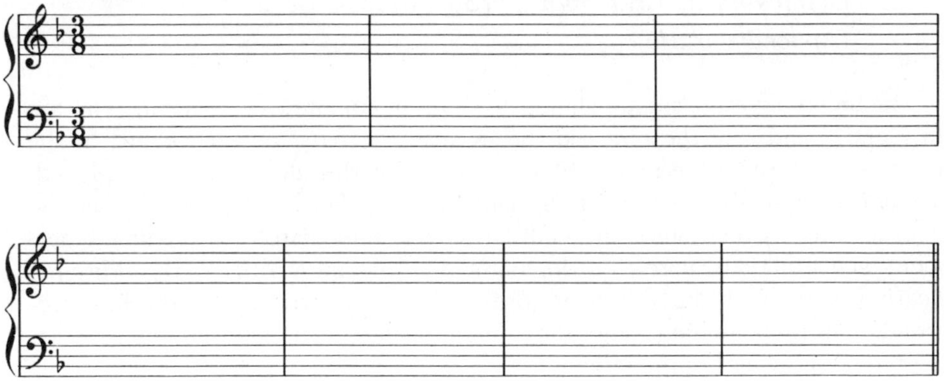

25.

Vivaldi, *Domine Deus*

Largo

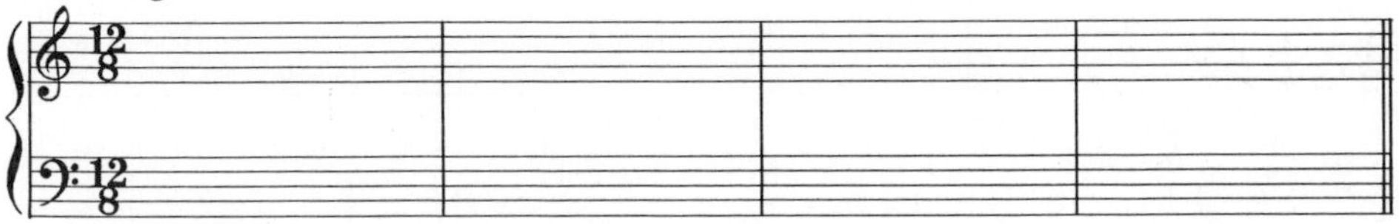

26.

Brahms, *Requiem,* III

Poco animato

28.

29.

Two-Voice Dictation

(*Appendix, p. 248*)

Listen to each excerpt completely, noting the chordal implications of this two-voice counterpoint. Write the Roman numerals under the bass clef (carefully observing inversions); then write the bass and soprano lines. The tonal center will be established before each exercise, but the tempo and meter must be inferred from the musical context. Ideally, two different instruments should be used for the dictation.

27.

Moderato

i   i 6   ___   ___   V   ___   ___

28.

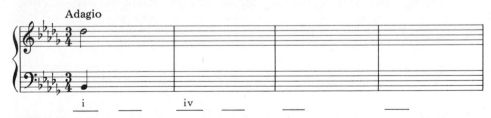

Adagio

i   ___   iv   ___   ___   ___

29.

Andante

i   ___   i 6   ___   iv   ___   ___

30.

Andantino

_____ i6 _____ _____ _____ iv6 _____ _____ V7 _____

31.

Vivaldi, *Laudamus Te (Gloria)*

Allegro

I _____ _____ _____ _____ _____ _____ _____ _____

Four-Voice Dictation

(*Appendix, p. 249*)

After the first hearing of each of the following excerpts, write the chord numerals below the bass clef. On subsequent hearings, notate the bass and soprano voices. If practical, add the alto and tenor voices later. The tempi will be mostly moderate, and the tonality will be established before each set of exercises in a common key. If the initial soprano and bass pitches are given, the tonality will not be established beforehand. Blanks indicate the number of chord changes per measure, but they are not always present in later exercises.

32.

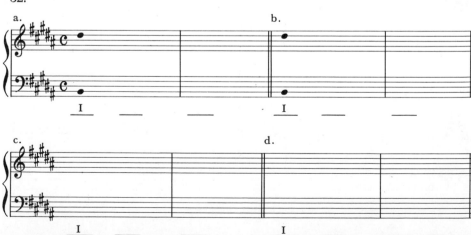

a.   b.

I _____ _____ _____   I _____ _____ _____

c.   d.

I _____ _____ _____   I _____ _____ _____

33.

a.   b.

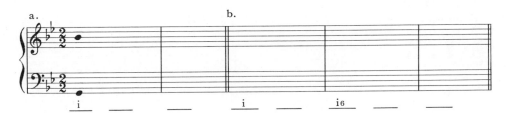

i ____ ____   i   ____   i6 ____ ____

c.

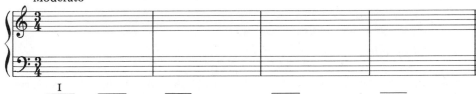

i   V7 ____ ____   i$^6_4$ ____

34.

Moderato

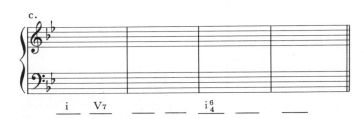

I ____ ____ ____ ____

35.

Andantino

____ ____ I6 ____ ____ I ____ ____

36.

Moderato

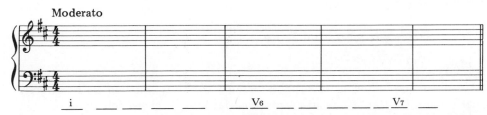

i ____ ____ ____ V6 ____ ____ ____ V7 ____

37.

Chopin, Mazurka, Op.7, No.1

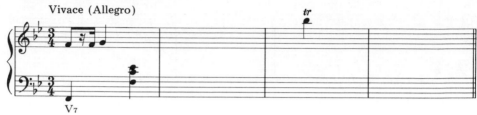

38.

Brahms, Op.119, No.4

Error Detection—Chord Series

(*Appendix, p. 251*)

Each of the following series of chord progressions will be played incorrectly. Raise your hand whenever you hear an error; then correct it if possible. Initially there will be no rhythm pattern (block chords only), and relatively few errors will appear. As the texture and rhythm become more complex, the errors increase.

39. D: I   V   I⁶   IV   V   I

40. F♯: I   V⁶   I   I⁶   IV   V⁷   I

41. d: i   V⁶   i   i⁶   iv   iv⁶   i   V⁷   i

42. A $\frac{3}{4}$ Moderato: I   IV   V │ I   V │ I   I⁶   IV⁶ │ V⁶   V   V⁷ │ I ‖

43. c♯ $\frac{3}{8}$ Andante: i   iv⁶ │ V   i   i⁶ │ iv   iv⁶ │ V   i $\frac{6}{4}$ V⁷ │ i ‖

44. D♭ $\frac{2}{2}$ Moderato: I   I⁶   IV │ I   IV   V │ IV⁶   V   I⁶ │
    IV⁶   V   I $\frac{6}{4}$ V⁷ │ I ‖

Error Detection from Score

(*Appendix, p. 253*)

Each of the following excerpts is notated correctly but will be incorrectly performed. On the first hearing, place a check mark over each error you observe. On subsequent hearings, identify the errors, notating them directly on the printed score. Errors may be in chord type, chord position, chord function (incorrect root), or rhythm. Suggested incorrect versions may be found in the Appendix, but inadvertent errors are equally valid. As an alternative procedure, stop the music when you hear an error and show the performer how **to** correct the error.

45.

Schubert, Sonata, Op.42, III

46.

Vivaldi, Cello Sonata No.3, III

47.

Haydn, Sonata No.43, II

48.

Schumann, Piano Concerto, Op.54, I

Allegro affettuoso

49.

Schubert, Sonata in A, II

Andantino

Error Detection by Memory

(*Appendix, p. 256*)

These exercises are similar to those first presented in Chapter XV. Carefully study each excerpt for a brief period, memorize it, and then determine whether or not the version played is correct by raising your hand whenever you believe an error occurs. If possible, correct the error; however, recognition is still more important than correction at this stage. After going once through the excerpt, correcting errors, you may reexamine the score; all subsequent playings will follow this reexamination of the score. Errors will occur only in chord type, chord position, or chord function, but not in rhythm or melody.

50.

51.

52.

53.

54.

XVIII

Suspension, Appoggiatura, and
Other Nonharmonic Tones
Motivic Development
Two-Voice Imitative Counterpoint

NONHARMONIC TONES

Much of the expressive character of tonal music results from the skillful use of nonharmonic tones. We have already considered the passing tone and neighboring tone, the two most commonly encountered nonharmonic tones, as well as the anticipation, and in this chapter we will examine other kinds of dissonant tones. Of these, the two most common are the suspension and the appoggiatura.

The *suspension* is an emphasized dissonance occurring between the bass (usually) and some other voice, which resolves to a more consonant interval on a less emphasized beat. The pitch to be suspended as a dissonance is "prepared," appearing first as a consonant member of the previous harmony, then as a dissonant "suspension," and finally resolving by step as a consonant "resolution." The most common suspensions are the dissonant intervals 4 resolving to 3, 7 to 6, 9 to 8, or 2 to 3 (the latter being the only common suspension in which the bass acts as the dissonant suspended tone).

FIGURE 1: SUSPENSIONS

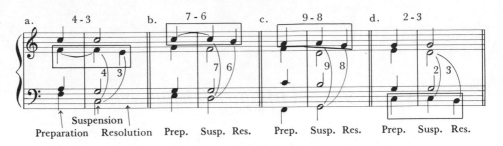

Note that all the specimen suspensions occur on the strong beat, followed, on a weaker beat, by the consonant resolution. Note also that the suspensions in Figure 1a and b̭ are tied across the bar line, while 1c and d are not tied. Whether tied or not, the process is the same, and all dissonances following this process may be regarded as suspensions, though a few theorists prefer to regard an untied suspension as an "appoggiatura."

The *appoggiatura* is also an emphasized dissonance but is not prepared in the same voice, as is the case with suspension. The appoggiatura resolves by step—usually down—and may be approached by either skip or step. The dissonance is more piquant than the consonant resolution and in most tonal music is sustained longer than the resolution (or at least as long). The "standard" appoggiatura is approached by skip and left by step, as in Figure 2a, but other configurations occur frequently (2b–d).

FIGURE 2: APPOGGIATURA

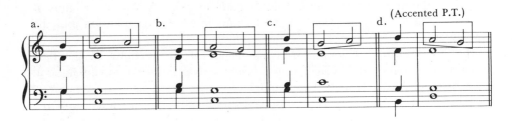

Note that in 2d the dissonance occurs in the course of consecutive stepwise motion (down, in this instance), which in all respects resembles the passing tone pattern, except that the dissonance occurs here on an emphasized, rather than unemphasized, beat. This appoggiatura figure is often referred to as the "accented passing tone."

Occasionally two dissonant notes precede the note of resolution, forming the upper and lower neighbors of the note of resolution. This figure is the *double appoggiatura.*

FIGURE 3: DOUBLE APPOGGIATURA

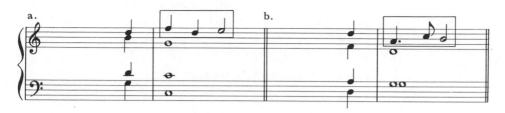

Most dissonances can occur simultaneously in more than one voice, as in the passing tone, neighboring tone, and appoggiatura patterns in Figure 4.

FIGURE 4: SIMULTANEOUS DISSONANCE

Miscellaneous Dissonance Patterns

Three other dissonance patterns, all normally unemphasized, are the *escape tone* (échappée), the *double neighboring tone* (DNT), and the *cambiata*. The first two patterns are relatively simple, and most theorists agree upon their handling, notwithstanding slight differences of terminology.

The *escape tone* (échappée) is a three-note figure with an unemphasized dissonance occurring between two consonant tones, moving in the opposite direction of the consonant movement. Usually the pattern exhibits a step-skip interval structure.

FIGURE 5: ESCAPE TONE (ÉCHAPPÉE)

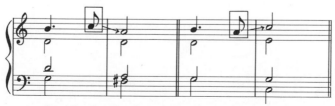

Opposite the direction of the consonant resolution

The double neighboring tone (DNT—also double auxiliary) is a four-note pattern involving the consecutive use of both upper and lower neighboring tones between the same starting and ending pitch. This pattern is found more frequently in instrumental or keyboard music than in vocal music.

FIGURE 6: DOUBLE NEIGHBORING TONES

The *cambiata* pattern has been used commonly since the time of the early Renaissance, though theorists differ more on details of its usage than on the use of other nonharmonic tones. In its simplest form it is a three-note figure, in essence the reverse of the escape tone, with the dissonance moving in the same direction as the consonant movement, rather than against it, as in the escape tone. In this form, it follows a skip-step pattern.

FIGURE 7: THREE–NOTE CAMBIATA

In the direction of the consonant resolution

The traditional cambiata pattern in use since the Renaissance is a four-note figure (some theorists say five) involving two unemphasized dissonances (or one, depending upon intervallic context).

FIGURE 8: TRADITIONAL CAMBIATA PATTERN

2-note dissonance   Single dissonance

The cambiata pattern in its traditional form and the double neighboring tone pattern are also referred to as *changing tones* (changing notes, changing note group).

PERFORMING

The following exercises are intended to be sung, preferably, or played, as examples of these various dissonance figures. Concentrate upon each dissonance and resolution as it occurs; to a lesser extent, perhaps, consider also the approach to the dissonance. If performed individually, the lower part should be played on the piano as the upper line is sung.

Suspensions

1.

2.

Appoggiature

(Dissonances in parentheses are relatively mild.)

3.

Miscellaneous

4.

5.

6. Analyze; then perform.

LISTENING

Melodic Dictation

(*Appendix, p. 259*)

Dissonances are heard, of course, in relation to a particular chord or implied harmony, so single-line melodic dictation involving nonharmonic tones is not technically viable. The next excerpts, however, are short and relatively simple exercises in melodic dictation, each of which exhibits contour and rhythm patterns typical of the dissonance figures under consideration. The actual dissonance with another line has been eliminated to permit sharper focus on the melodic character of various dissonant tones. As you listen, pay particular attention to the implied dissonances and their subsequent resolutions. Though you have encountered similar melodic gestures before, from this time on be particularly aware of the potential differences in function (nonharmonic tone vs. chord tone) among various pitches in the same melody. As always, listen to the entire excerpt before writing. The initial pitch or opening figure is given. Check your answers with the melodies given in the Appendix.

Appoggiature

7.

Alla marcia

8.

Moderato

Suspensions

9.

Andante con moto

10.

Allegro moderato

Miscellaneous

11.

Briskly

12.

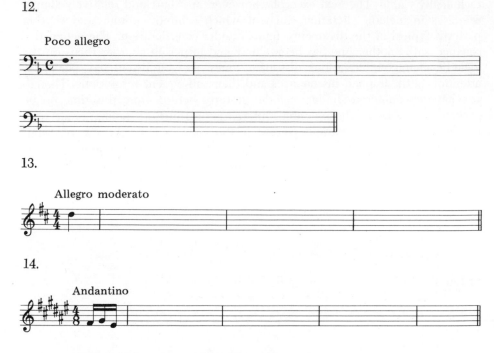

13.

14.

Melodic Dictation with a Given Bass

(Appendix, p. 260)

In these exercises you are to write the missing melodic line after each excerpt is played. The line will form frequent dissonances with the given voice (or voices). In certain of the exercises you will be asked to fill in a line (or lines) other than the soprano. Be aware of the characteristic dissonance patterns and their resolutions at the same time as you concentrate upon the horizontal aspects of the melody. The longer exercises should be divided into more digestible segments after the exercise is played completely through once. The segments may be repeated, but not too often. Since the tonality of each exercise can be deduced readily from the partially-notated score, neither the key nor the tempo need be established before each exercise.

15.

16.

Allegretto

17.

Bach

(Andante)

18.

Mozart, Sonata, K.333, I

Allegro

19.

Mozart, K.332, I

Allegro

20.

Bach

MOTIVIC DEVELOPMENT

Often a melody of considerable length will be spun from relatively short fragments which are repeated, transposed, extended, varied, or otherwise developed by the composer. Such constructive fragments (or building blocks, or germ cells), commonly referred to as *motives,* were introduced earlier in Chapter XIV. It is important to recognize the presence of a motive when one is heard prominently in a composition and to anticipate and follow the motive as it is developed. New repetitions, transpositions, or variations of a motive often mark the beginnings (occasionally the ends) of phrases, semi-phrases, or periods, and significant changes of motive (or theme) often separate larger sections of a composition one from another. The technique involved in the treatment of motives is a significant factor in distinguishing one composer's style from another, even within the same historical style period.

Naturally, a motive may be manipulated by a composer any way he chooses to create the particular effect he desires, with perhaps as many as twenty or thirty different manifestations occurring during the course of a single composition.

Several standard techniques of motivic development are commonly employed by composers, and are useful to consider as examples of motivic treatment.

Generally, motives may be developed by either mechanical or organic treatment. Mechanical treatment may be applied to any motive; organic treatment is unique to a particular motive, being dependent upon its particular rhythm, contour, and intervallic structure.

Mechanical Development

The original motive (a) in Figure 9 is first transposed (b), then presented in a series of transpositions called a sequence (c), then shown upside down (inversion—d), backwards (retrograde—e), and backwards and upside down (retrograde inversion—f), with faster note values (diminution—g), and slower note values (augmentation—h). In all instances the original motive is unchanged in terms of its interval relationships but has as an entity been subjected to a uniform modification.

FIGURE 9

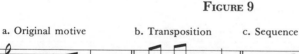

Organic Development

It is somewhat more difficult to categorize organic treatment, since it is always unique in every situation, but four general procedures are often used—development by the addition of material (at the beginning, middle, or end—a), by the deletion of material (b), by the varying of material (either the rhythm, contour, or intervallic structure of the original motive—c), or by a combination of factors (d).

FIGURE 10

a. Development by addition (expansion, enlargement)

1. At the beginning (prefix) 2. In the middle 3. At the end (suffix)

b. Development by deletion (contraction, compression, thinning)

1. At the beginning 2. In the middle 3. At the end

c. Development by variation

1. Interval change 2. Contour change

a. b. a. b.

3. Rhythm change

a. b.

d. Development by a combination of means

1. 2.

3.

Improvisation with Motives

Following are a few basic motives of varying length and character. Sing each one (or play it) and develop it using a variety of techniques similar to those already considered. When sufficiently confident, spin out a short motive into a phrase, ending with a satisfying cadence. Later, invent your own motives, or extract them from literature with which you are currently working and develop them similarly. The more readily you can manipulate motives yourself, even just mechanically, the more aware you will be of the way other composers handle motives, and your sensitivity to musical meaning will increase both as a performer and as a listener.

PERFORMING

21.

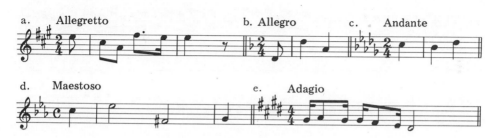

22.

LISTENING

Motivic Error Detection

(Appendix, p. 263)

Most of the melodies printed below will be played incorrectly. All derive from an important initial motive developed with a variety of techniques. Stop the music when you hear an error and give instructions to correct it. After each error is corrected, the playing will resume with the error corrected according to your instructions.

23.

Allegro molto

24.

25.

26.

27.

28.

29.

Mozart, Sonata, K.284, III

30.

Mozart, Sonata, K.284, III

31.

Mozart, Sonata, K.332, III

32.

Brahms, Intermezzo, Op.119, No.2

33.

Brahms, Rhapsody, Op.79, No.2

34.

Brahms, Intermezzo, Op.117, No.3

TWO-VOICE IMITATIVE COUNTERPOINT

The two-voice counterpoint encountered thus far in the text has consisted of two contrasting lines, generally complementary to one another in terms of both rhythm and melody. Composers just as frequently choose to unify the two lines by having them share common material, with important motives exchanged or "imitated" between the lines. The rhythm at any given moment is still largely complementary, but the melodic motives are shared alternately. The listener tends to focus on each new entrance of a motive as being the important musical idea of the moment, and his attention therefore shifts back and forth between the lines, depending upon which has the more recent entrance of the important motive. He hears imitative counterpoint "diagonally," alternating between the lines, whereas with nonimitative counterpoint, he tends to choose one line as the more important, or listens to the vertical relationships between equally important melodies.

FIGURE 11

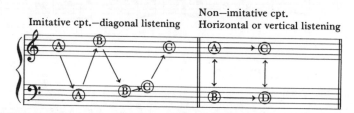

Imitative cpt.—diagonal listening

Non-imitative cpt.
Horizontal or vertical listening

If the imitation is exact, the lines are in "canon." Most imitation, however, is less strict, with changes of either rhythm or melody between the lines.

LISTENING

Dictation with Notated Signposts

(*Appendix, p. 266*)

Listen for motivic relationships between the lines, for dissonant intervals and their resolution, for tendency tones, rests, and complementary rhythms. The passages may be repeated by agreement, and, if necessary, longer passages may be broken into shorter segments.

35.

Allegro

36.

37.

38.

Josquin des Prez, *Pleni Sunt Coeli (Missa L'Homme Arme)*

39.

Brahms, Symphony No.2, I

Dictation without Notated Signposts
(*Appendix, p. 268*)

The initial pitch or pitches, but not necessarily the initial rhythm pattern, will be given for each of the exercises. Listen to the complete excerpt, particularly to motivic exchanges, before beginning to write. The key and tempo may be established beforehand, but preferably this will be avoided.

40.

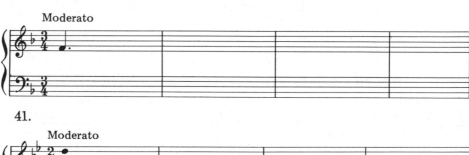

41.

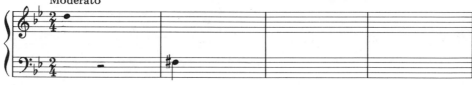

42.

43.

44.

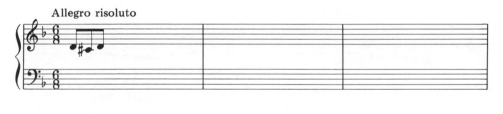

45.

Haydn, "The Lord is Great" *(The Creation)*

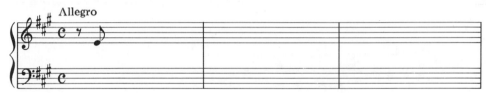

Error Detection

(Appendix, p. 269)

The following excerpts, printed correctly below, will be performed with errors. Either stop the music when you hear an error and correct it immediately, or make a check mark over each passage where an error occurs and later notate the errors directly on the score, using a colored pencil. Errors will occur in either or both the rhythm and the melody, and either in a series or individually. Listen for the errors in series first, then concentrate on single errors. Neither tempo nor key will be established beforehand.

46.

Bach, Two-part Inventions, I
(Poco allegro)

47.

Haydn, "Achieved is the Glorious Word" *(The Creation)*

Vivace (Allegro)

48.

Bach, Fugue 1, *The Well-Tempered Clavier,* Vol. I

(Poco adagio)

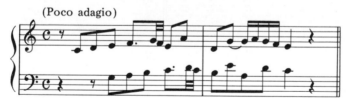

49.

D.Scarlatti, Sonata in A minor (Kirkpatrick No. 3)

(Allegro moderato)

50.

Beethoven, String Quartet, Op.131, I

Adagio, ma non troppo e molto espressivo

51.

Adapted from Corelli, Trio Sonata, II

Presto (Allegro)

52.

Bach, Two-part Invention, VI

XIX

Inversions of the Dominant Seventh

Secondary Triads

More Chord Patterns

THE DOMINANT SEVENTH

The dominant seventh chord has been encountered frequently since Chapter XV, and various aspects of its resolution have been explored in considerable detail. When the chord is inverted and outlined from the bottom up, all four pitches are retained, but the characteristic interval of the minor seventh between root and seventh disappears, replaced by the characteristic interval of a major second—the inversion of the seventh. The location of the characteristic second interval is one means of determining (aurally) the particular inversion of the chord. If the second is on top, the chord is in first inversion; if in the middle, the chord is in second inversion; if on the bottom the chord is in third inversion. This is similar to the inversions of a simple triad, in which, however, the fourth is the characteristic interval that determines the inversion. If the fourth is on top, the triad is in first inversion; if on the bottom, the triad is in second inversion. To generalize, then, for all chord inversions, if the characteristic interval is on top, the chord is in first inversion; if on the bottom, the chord is in its last possible inversion.

Naturally, inversions of the dominant seventh may be spaced in a variety of ways depending upon the context, and in certain spacings the characteristic second interval is not readily apparent. In such contexts one must rely on identifying the chord factor in the bass—the third of the chord (the leading tone) will indicate first inversion, the fifth will indicate second inversion, and the seventh will indicate third inversion. Both methods used in support of one another will provide flexibility in identifying inversions; in certain contexts either one or the other may prove more useful.

The inversions normally resolve to some form of the tonic triad with the same voice leading as found in the V⁷ in root position—the leading tone resolving upward to the tonic, and the chord seventh resolving down to the third of the tonic. Other resolutions are possible, but this standard resolution should be regarded as the norm.

Figure 1

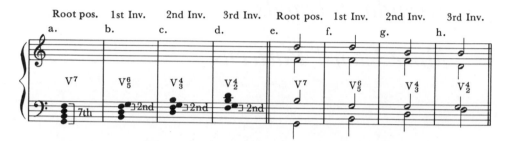

Figure 2

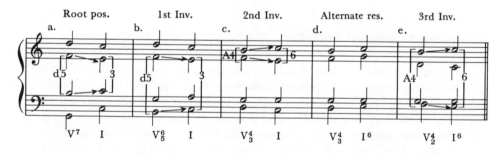

Note that in all the resolutions in Figure 2, when the tritone interval always present in the dominant seventh is expressed as a diminished fifth, the resolution is inward to a third; when it is expressed as an augmented fourth, the resolution is outward to a sixth. This phenomenon may be expanded to a general principle: diminished intervals normally resolve inward; augmented intervals resolve outward (an exception may be noted above in Figure 2-d, in the alternate resolution of the V$\frac{4}{3}$ to the I⁶). The chord seventh, contrary to its tendency, resolves upward rather than down, and the augmented fourth interval consequently does not resolve outward. When *any* seventh chord resolves to any other chord in first inversion, voice leading contrary to the normal resolution of the seventh may occur and may be regarded as the "normal" exception.

As you perform the following introductory exercises, pay particular attention to the location of the characteristic interval of the second, to the presence and resolution of the leading tone, and to the expansion or contraction of the tritone. Note that the standard resolution of the V $\frac{4}{2}$ (or V²) is to the I⁶, not to the I in root position. Remember also that a dominant seventh (or its inversions) will be constructed the same whether it exists in a major or minor key, resolving to a major or minor tonic, respectively.

PERFORMING

1.

V_5^6—I

2.

V_3^4—I

Move up by half steps through other keys.

3.

V_3^4—I⁶

4.

V_2^4—I⁶

5.

V_5^6—I   Allegro (in 1)

Move by half steps through other keys.

6.

V_3^4—i

7.

LISTENING

Identification of Inversions

(*Appendix, p. 275*)

9– Identify the dominant seventh inversion employed in each of these three-
10. chord progressions. The tonality will be established before each exercise. Listen to the bass note and to the location of the second.

11– Raise your hand when you identify the specified progression in each
12. of the following exercises (i.e., V²–I⁶, etc.). The particular progression should be announced before each exercise is played. As an alternative procedure, identify each position of a dominant seventh inversion you hear. The tonality will be established before each exercise.

SECONDARY TRIADS

Aural identification of chords is relatively uncomplicated when only the three primary triads are used. From the tonic, a progression normally moves (sooner or later) to the dominant, whereupon it returns to the tonic. The subdominant, when present, often precedes the dominant, serving as a connector between tonic and dominant. In much tonal music, the primary triads predominate, and the four diatonic secondary triads are employed for purposes of variety, each of them serving as an alternate for one of the primary triads and normally used more sparingly than the primary triads. Of all the secondary triads, the supertonic is the most frequently, and in certain works may be used even more frequently than the subdominant, especially in cadence progressions. Thus the supertonic and the subdominant (ii and IV) are interchangeable at cadence points. The balance between the use of primary triads in relation to secondary triads varies somewhat from composer to composer and is one of the distinguishing features of a composer's personal style.

A composer selects a chord for use at any given moment principally on the basis of its function within the desired progression. Each of the three primary triads is in a different functional category, and for each primary triad there is a secondary triad with a root a third lower which serves as an alternate chord within the same functional category. Thus the tonic category consists of the I and vi; the subdominant consists of the IV and ii; and the dominant consists of all the chords that contain the leading tone—the V, vii°, and iii. The dominant-tonic relationship is the strongest functional relationship underlying all tonal music.

FIGURE 3: CHORD FUNCTIONS

	Tonic	Subdominant	Dominant	Tonic	Subdominant
Primary Triad:	I ↓	IV ↓	V ↑	I ↓	IV ↓
Secondary Triad:	vi	ii	vii°	vi	ii
			iii		

The normal progression from category to category in the chart under Figure 3 is from left to right, regardless of whether a primary triad or secondary triad is used. If a chord change is made *within* a category, the normal progression is from a primary triad to a secondary triad, rather than the reverse. A chord change in which the root progresses *down* by a third sounds stronger than one in which it progresses *up* by a third, because the root of the second chord *is not* a common tone in the first chord when the root *descends,* but *is* a common tone when the root *ascends.* Note that the primary and secondary triads in each functional category share two tones in common, which accounts for their similarity of sound and function.

The most common chord progressions are those in which the root progresses up by a fourth (as in the progression V–I or ii–V) or a fifth (as in I–V or IV–I), or down a third (I–vi or vi–IV). Progressions up a third (ii–IV or iii–V) are usually weaker, and progressions up or down by a second, having no tones in common and always occurring *between* functional categories, are striking and exhibit strong contrasts.

In summary, then, the most common strong chord progressions occur between chords whose roots are a fourth or a fifth apart. Between such chords there is a single common tone that provides a sense of unity, and two tones that are different, producing a sense of variety. Between chords a third apart there will be two common tones, and the chords will sound more alike than different. Between chords a step apart, there will be no common tones, and the chords will sound totally dissimilar.

Chord function is an area of theory in which there is wide disagreement, and no commonly accepted formulae exist that ensure good harmony for the student composer under all conditions or that explain all the procedures found in standard literature. The chart in Figure 3 and the remarks above are generalizations therefore, more accurate than not in most contexts, but neither universally applicable nor universally desirable. A patient and understanding theory teacher can do much at this stage to help the anxious student grasp the principles of good chord choice, yet savor the freedom of multiple possibilities available to him in most situations. Good chord choice is aesthetic aptness, and primarily a facet of the art—as opposed to the science—of music.

As you perform the following exercises, pay particular attention to two things: (1) changes of chord function and especially motion into the cadence, and (2) the relationship of common tones between chords (or lack of common tones).

PERFORMING

Linear Chord Changes

13.

14.

15.

16.

17.

Aural Determination of Secondary Triads

Major Keys: The ii, iii, and vi are all minor triads, contrasting strongly in quality with the primary triads, which are major chords. The vii° is a diminished triad in both major and minor keys, just as V is normally a major chord in both modes. Thus the important dominant-functioning triads remain constant whatever the mode.

FIGURE 4

If the tonic degree is heard in a minor triad, the chord is the vi. If the leading tone is present in a minor triad, the chord is the iii. If the leading tone is present in a diminished triad, the chord is the vii°. If neither tonic nor leading tone is present in a minor triad, the chord is the ii. The key melodic focal points are the tonic and the leading tone, the most readily remembered pitches in any given tonality. These two pitches are the key to relating chord quality (major, minor, diminished, augmented, etc.) to chord function (vi, IV, I, etc.)

Minor keys: Distinguishing secondary triads in minor keys is somewhat more complex, since there is a greater variety of chord types possible. In general, assume the chord types formed on a harmonic minor scale to be the norm. The principal triads i and iv are minor in quality, while V is major (and vii° is diminished, as previously noted in the major key). The ii° chord is also diminished, while VI is major. Both chords are used prominently in the minor mode. The III⁺ chord, augmented in quality, is rarely encountered, and when found, almost always progresses to the VI chord.

FIGURE 5

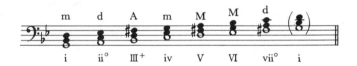

If the tonic degree is present in a major triad, the chord is the VI. If the leading tone is present in an augmented triad, the chord is the III⁺; if present in a diminished triad, the chord is the vii°. If a diminished triad is heard without either tonic or leading tone, the chord is the ii°. The tonic and leading tone remain the most important melodic focal points.

If the upper tetrachord of the melodic minor scale forms the basis for harmonization, other chord types occur. Only two (or three) such variant chords are commonly encountered; the others appear only occasionally or rarely. The common variants occur as the result of harmonization of the *descending* form of the melodic minor scale (the natural, or pure minor) and appear as a major triad on ♭VII (the subtonic), a major triad on III (the major mediant), or occasionally as a minor triad on v (the minor dominant). In minor keys, there is frequent harmonic motion toward III (as the area of the relative major—of which the major triad on the subtonic [♭VII] is the dominant). These common variants—the major triads on III and VII, and, slightly less important, the minor triad on v—should be practiced regularly, along with the standard triads formed on the harmonic minor scale.

The other variants—a minor triad on ii, a major triad on IV, and a diminished triad on vi°—all formed from the harmonization of the *ascending* form of the melodic minor scale, will be far less frequently encountered.

Figure 6 shows the various possible types of triads in a minor key, with the most common *variants* in bold face notation. Note that only the tonic chord exists in a single form—as a minor triad.

FIGURE 6

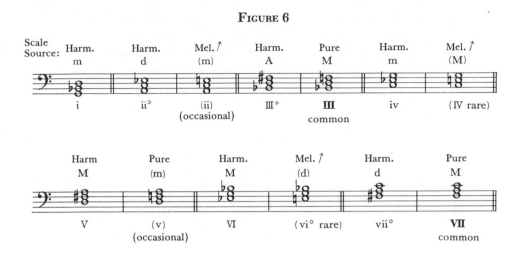

PERFORMING

Chord Outlining

18. As a means of increasing awareness of the various roles a bass note may play in different chords within the same key, outline all three triads to which each bass note could belong within any given key. Use letter names preferably (B-D♯-F♯) or a neutral vowel. Special attention should be paid to minor keys, which exhibit more possible variations than major keys.

FIGURE 7

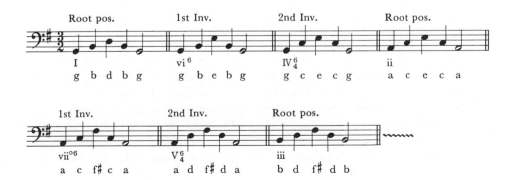

19. Establish a key, either major or minor. At a comfortable pace, with even pulses, sing the *bass* line only of the following progressions. Use a neutral vowel or, preferably, sing the specific letter name of each pitch. The object of the exercise is to focus attention on the bass line of a chord progression—the primary determinant of chord function. In minor keys, as a general procedure, use the harmonic minor scale as the basis for the progression, employing the upper tetrachord of the melodic minor scale (in both forms) only for variety, and only when appropriate. Particular attention should be paid to minor keys, since they are usually harder for most students.

Example

FIGURE 8

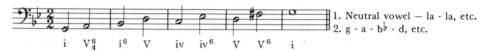

i   V$^6_4$ i^6 V   iv   iv^6 V   V^6 i

1. Neutral vowel — la - la, etc.
2. g - a - b♭ - d, etc.

Major keys:

a. I   IV   ii   V   IV   vi   V   V^6 I

b. I   V^6 vi   IV   I^6 vi   V   iii   ii^6 V^6 I

c. I   iii   IV   ii   V^6 vi^6 vii$^{\circ 6}$ I^6 IV   V   I

Minor keys:

d. i   iv   ii   i^6 VI   iv   III^{+6} i^6 ii$^{\circ 6}$ V   i

e. i   VII   VI   V   ii$^{\circ 6}$ i$^6_4$ iv^6 ii$^\circ$ i^6 vii$^{\circ 6}$ i

f. i   V^6 VI^6 vii$^{\circ 6}$ i^6 VI   iv   i$^6_4$ iv^6 V   i^6 V$^6_4$ i   V^6 V   i

Invent other similar progressions.

20. Outline triads from the bass up (and down again) according to the chord numerals given in the following series (see sample progression in Figure 9 below). Maintain a steady tempo, singing either on a neutral vowel or using letter names. It is useful for someone to sit at the piano, checking the chords occasionally for accuracy of intonation. Change the meter as necessary to adjust to the particular situation. After performing the following series, invent other series with Red calling out chord numerals as Blue outlines the chords, leading eventually to a V–I cadence; or, having analyzed a progression in a piece of music literature, use that progression for outlining.

FIGURE 9

Progression: I vii°⁶ I⁶ IV V I

Major keys:

I   IV   ii   V   vi   ii⁶   V   i

I   V $\frac{6}{4}$ I⁶   IV   ii⁶   V   vi   I $\frac{6}{4}$ V⁷   I

I   V $\frac{4}{3}$ I⁶   V²   I⁶   vii°⁶   iii   vi   V   I

I   V $\frac{6}{5}$ I   vi   ii⁶   iii⁶   vi   IV   I⁶   V $\frac{4}{3}$ I

I   vi   IV   V   V⁶   vi⁶   ii   V   vi   V $\frac{6}{5}$ vi⁶   ii⁶   V⁷   I

Minor keys:

i   iv   V   VI   ii°⁶   V²   i⁶   vii°⁶   i

i   V $\frac{6}{5}$ i   i⁶   vii°⁶   ii°⁶   i⁶   V   VI   iv   I $\frac{6}{4}$ V   i

I   III⁺   VI   iv⁶   V   V²   i⁶   iv   V   V $\frac{6}{5}$ i

i   V   VI   iv   ii°   VI⁶   iv   i $\frac{6}{4}$ V   VI   ii°⁶   V   V⁷   i

i   VII   VI   V   VI   ii°⁶   V   III   VI   III⁶   ii°⁶   i⁶   V $\frac{6}{4}$ i   iv   i

21. Blue establishes a given tonality, then announces a chord (e.g., IV⁶). Blue then plays a series of random chords in the key, only one of which is the stated chord. Red identifies the stated chord when he hears it. *Variant:* Outline each random chord after it has been played; then identify it by chord number.

LISTENING

Chord Identification

(*Appendix, p. 277*)

22– Before each of the following series is played, a single chord or single
26. progression will be announced. Identify that chord or progression whenever you hear it. Whenever an incorrect response occurs, begin again.

PERFORMING

27. Four individuals, or groups of people, are needed for the following exercise, each to sing a different part. They will be given the specific spacing of the initial chord and the chord numerals of the progression. Using only the chord numerals, and without referring to the progression written out in notation, they are to sing, with proper voice leading and doubling, the desired progression. The tempo should be comfortably slow and even throughout. With increased skill, the tempo may be accelerated. The voice leading should be critically observed by all other listeners, and corrected as errors occur. Use letter names, preferably, or a neutral vowel.

Suggested progressions:

G: I V^6 I iii IV V I   g: i V VI iv i$^6_4$ V^7 i   b: i V$^6_4$i^6 iv i$^6_4$ V^{7}VI V i

d: i V$^6_5$ i V$^4_3$ i^6 iv V V$^6_5$ i   E: I IV I$^6_4$ IV^6 V^6 vi^6 IV V I   e: i VI iv ii^{o6} V V$^6_5$ i iv i

e♭: i VI ii^{o6} III iv i$^6_4$ VI V i   D: I V$^6_5$ I vi I$^6_4$ V^7 vi vii^o I   F: I IV^6 V^6 I vii^{o6} I^{6}ii^6 I$^6_4$ V^7 I

The Deceptive Cadence

A favorite harmonic device of composers is the deceptive cadence, a closing progression in which the listener is led to expect a V–I cadence but in which the dominant chord resolves instead to a chord other than the tonic—most often the vi chord. The deceptive cadence is often followed closely by a true authentic cadence, as if to point up the harmonic deception. Figure 10 shows a typical setting.

FIGURE 10

C: I   vii°⁶ I⁶   ii⁶   I⁶₄   V   vi   IV   I⁶₄   V⁷   I

MORE CHORD PATTERNS

Several chord patterns (stock progressions) have been identified in previous chapters, and several exercises in Chapter XVII were devoted to the recognition of five patterns—the cadential ⁶₄, (I ⁶₄ V I), the neighboring chord pattern (I V⁶ I, V IV⁶ V, etc.) and progressive patterns I I⁶ IV, I IV V I, and I I⁶ IV IV⁶ V V⁶ I (the latter an obvious variant of the previous pattern).

The ⁶₄ chord, being relatively distinctive in quality yet limited in usage, is normally approached and left by either common tone or step, and consequently falls into predictable patterns. In addition to the cadential progression, the ⁶₄ is frequently handled in two other ways—in a passing progression and in a pedal progression. Other usages may be found, of course, but these two are the most commonly encountered and the most aurally predictable.

PERFORMING

The Passing ⁶₄

In this progression, the bass line moves by stepwise motion continuously up or down through three different pitches, the second of which connects the outer pitches in the manner of a passing tone. This second bass pitch is harmonized with a ⁶₄ chord, serving as a connecting chord between a triad in root position and in first inversion. More often than not, the connecting ⁶₄ chord will occur on an unemphasized beat. Practice the next exercise in several different major and minor keys, using a variety of different chords in similar patterns.

28.

$$\text{I} \quad \text{V}^6_4 \quad \text{I}^6 \qquad \text{I}^6 \quad \text{V}^6_4 \quad \text{I} \qquad \text{ii} \quad \text{vi}^6_4 \quad \text{ii}^6 \qquad \text{ii}^6 \quad \text{vi}^6_4 \quad \text{ii} \qquad \text{iv} \quad \text{i}^6_4 \quad \text{iv}^6 \qquad \text{iv}^6 \quad \text{i}^6_4 \quad \text{iv}$$

The Pedal $^6_4$ (Stationary, Auxiliary)

In this progression involving three chords, the bass note remains stationary throughout. Again the second chord is the $^6_4$, functioning as an auxiliary chord to the chords on either side. As with the passing $^6_4$, the $^6_4$ chord is normally unemphasized.

29.

$$\text{I} \quad \text{IV}^6_4 \quad \text{I} \qquad \text{I} \quad \text{IV}^6_4 \quad \text{I} \qquad \text{V} \quad \text{i}^6_4 \quad \text{V} \qquad \text{V} \quad \text{i}^6_4 \quad \text{V}$$

V^2-I^6 Progression

Inversion of the V^7 are versatile chords, occurring in numerous different and often unpredictable contexts. The third inversion, however, with its customary resolution to I^6, is both distinctive and predictable. The bass of the V^2 chord is normally (but not always) approached by common tone or step (from above) and resolves down by step. The other voices sometimes move irregularly, but the bass line remains constant. In minor keys especially, irregular voice leading may be necessary to avoid awkward intervals.

30.

$$\text{IV} \quad \text{V}^4_2 \quad \text{I}^6 \qquad \text{ii}^6 \quad \text{V}^4_2 \quad \text{I}^6 \qquad \text{iv} \quad \text{V}^4_2 \quad \text{i}^6 \qquad \text{V} \quad ^4_2 \quad \text{i}^6$$

I-iii -IV Progression

In major keys, when the soprano melody descends by step from the tonic, the stock progression I-iii-IV may be used effectively to harmonize the first three notes of the descending soprano. If the tonic soprano note is sustained while the bass changes below, the next soprano note may be heard as a passing tone. In either situation, the iii chord serves as a connecting chord between the I and the IV.

31.

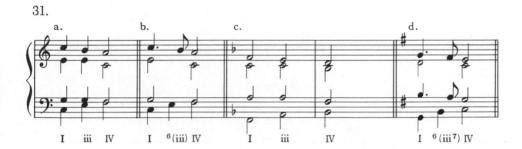

Consecutive First Inversion (Fauxbourdon) Progression

Successive chords in first inversion have been part of the common harmonic vocabulary since the fifteenth century. In this progression, the bass always moves in parallel sixths with the soprano in either ascending or descending motion. An inside voice usually moves in parallel fourths with the soprano, while the fourth voice, when present, reverses the pitch order of the bass line (32 a, b). If this voice leading is strictly continued beyond three chords, a dissonant clash or an overlap will occur, so some adjustment must be made after three chords (32 c). In minor keys, awkward augmented intervals may occur if harmonic minor is used melodically (32 d); therefore the melodic minor scale (descending natural minor) will often be harmonized to avoid such skips (32 e). As you practice Exercise 32 with a variety of keys, chords, and initial spacings, listen for the constant interval of a sixth between bass and soprano, the latter of which will always function as the root of the chord.

32.

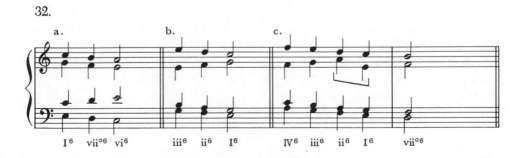

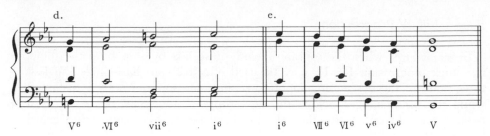

$$V^6 \quad \text{.VI}^6 \quad \text{vii}^6 \qquad i^6 \qquad i^6 \quad \text{VII}^6 \text{ VI}^6 \text{ v}^6 \text{ iv}^6 \quad V$$

Of course it is possible to write a progression such as I⁶–ii⁶–iii⁶–IV⁶ in which the soprano does not move in parallel sixths with the bass, but such a progression is a deliberate exception to the normal procedure, which is designed to emphasize the parallel relationship between bass and soprano.

FIGURE 11

$$I^6 \qquad ii^6 \qquad iii^6 \qquad IV^6$$

ii–V Progression

The ii chord is the most common secondary triad and appears as an equal (substitute) partner of the IV chord. To many listeners, the ii chord darkens the progression to V, both in major and minor keys. In major keys it is a minor chord, whereas IV is major; in minor keys ii° is a diminished triad, whereas iv is minor. Though ii shares a common tone with the V chord, often this bond is deliberately ignored as if there were no common tone, and ii progresses to V in contrary motion as in the progression IV to V. Compare the progressions ii-V and IV-V in Exercise 33, noting the darker color of the ii-V progression. Often the ii will resolve to a I $^6_4$ before pushing on to the dominant chord. However, this is still basically the same progression, since the I $^6_4$ chord in a cadence progression "leans" toward the dominant chord and demands resolution to it, as a result of the dissonant intervals of a sixth and fourth above the bass, which resolve to the stable fifth and third, respectively. Analyze, then perform, other cadence progressions involving either ii-V or IV-V, and substitute the opposite subdominant chord, noting the difference in sound.

33.

Descending Third Progression

Earlier in the chapter it was noted that the root movement of a descending third was a fairly common and strong progression, moving either between functional categories (vi-IV) or within a single category (I-vi). If all the chords are in root position, the descending motion in the bass is distinctive and fairly obvious. Such a progression could begin on any chord and end on any chord, so the following exercises are only illustrative, not definitive. Practice them in several keys and both major and minor modes.

34.

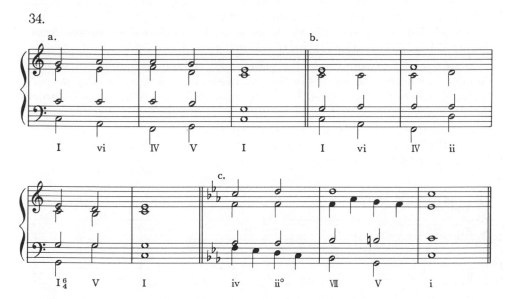

35.

i   VI   iv   ii°   vii°   V   i   iv⁶₄ i

LISTENING

Identification of a Specified Chord Pattern

(*Appendix, p. 278*)

36–
41. A particular chord pattern, or progression, will be specified at the beginning of each exercise. Raise your hand when you hear that pattern and lower it after the final chord of the progression. The key, tempo, and meter will *not* be established before each exercise, unless agreed upon to the contrary. The suggested series in the Appendix may be reused with focus on different chord progressions, and, as always, you are encouraged to develop other chord series for additional practice.

Determining Chord Roots

(*Appendix, p. 280*)

As a means of preparing for harmonic dictation involving all triads, sing the chord root (not necessarily the bass) of each chord as these progressions are played. Sound the root as soon as possible after the chord has been played; on a subsequent hearing write the chord numeral for each different chord. Finally, determine the exact position of each chord and write the proper Arabic numbers for the figured bass. The primary object is to recognize true chord changes (not just changes of position or texture) and determine the root of each new chord as quickly as possible. As before, treat the bass of a cadential I⁶₄ chord as the root. The key will not be established; always assume the initial chord to be the tonic.

42.

Andante

43.

44.

Bach, Chorale No.191

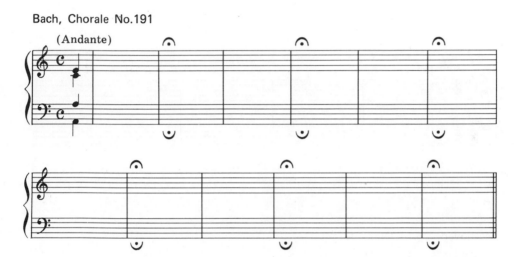

Four-Voice Dictation

(Appendix, p. 282)

Write the appropriate chord numerals below the bass clef as well as notating the soprano and bass voices. In most of the exercises, certain information will be given to you; in others, you must infer everything yourself. Whenever blanks are present below the bass clef, they indicate the number of chord changes in each measure. If there are no blanks, you are to determine this yourself as you write the chord numerals.

The object of these exercises is to correlate the chord function (Roman numerals) with the melodic lines in the soprano and bass. It does not matter whether you concentrate first on the harmonic aspects or the melodic aspects. Eventually you should listen to both aspects simultaneously since they are equally important, though at any given moment one or the other may predominate. Ultimately you should try to notate the tenor and alto lines also, but the outside lines are far more important in terms of musical flow.

The tonality will be established before each exercise in a new key.

45.

46.

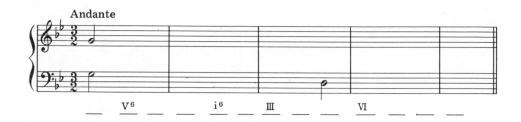

47.

Beethoven, Op.14, No.2, II

48.

Bach, Chorale No.257

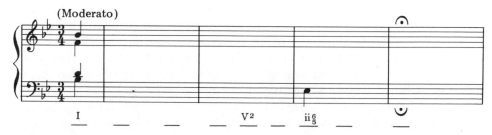

F $\lceil$ I⁶
$\lfloor$ IV⁶   V$^4_3$

49.

Beethoven, Op.2, No.3, II

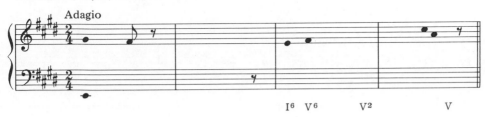

I⁶   V⁶   V²   V

50.

Beethoven, Op.2, No.2, II

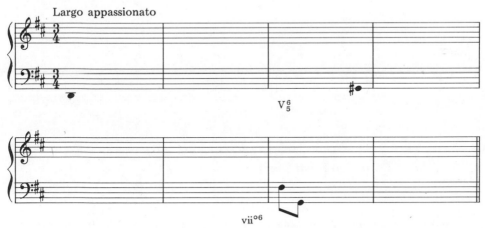

V$^6_5$

vii°⁶

Error Detection

(Appendix, p. 284)

Each of the following series of chord progressions will be played incorrectly. Raise your hand when you hear an error, then correct it if possible. Initially there will be no rhythmic patterns (block chords only), and relatively few errors will occur. As texture and rhythm become more complex, the errors will increase. The key, but not necessarily the tempo, will be established before each exercise.

51.

D: I   iii   vi   ii   V V^7 I

52.

b: i ii^{o6} V V^2 i^6 vii^{o6} i

53.

E♭:   I   vi   V   vi IV^6 I^6_4 ii^6 V^2 I^6 IV iii^6 V^7 I

54.

Allegro risoluto

A♭: $\frac{4}{4}$ I I^6 IV | IV^6 V^6 I | V V^7 ii IV^6 | I   IV I^6_4 V^7 | I   ‖

55.

Allegro

E♭: $\frac{4}{4}$ I   vi | IV I^6 | vii^{o6} I | vii^{o6} I^6 ii^{o6} V | vi | IV I^6 | ii   V | V^7 I   ‖

Error Detection From Score

(*Appendix, p. 286*)

Each of the following excerpts is correctly notated but will be incorrectly performed. Stop the music when you hear an error and correct the performer. It is also excellent practice to make a written response to the errors, making a check mark in the score over each error you hear and later notating the incorrect variants directly on the printed score with a colored pencil. The key and tempo should *not* be established before each excerpt is played.

56.

Mozart, Sonata, K.333, III

57.

Schubert, *Death and the Maiden,* II

58.

Beethoven, Sonata, Op.2, No.3, I

59.

60.

Brahms, Romance, Op.118, No.5

Error Detection by Memory

(*Appendix, p. 289*)

Carefully study each excerpt for a brief period, memorize it, and then raise your hand whenever you hear an error in the performance. Correct it if possible, but recognition of an error is still more important then correction by memory. After going through each excerpt once, correcting errors, you may reexamine the score; all subsequent hearings will follow this reexamination. Errors will occur in chord type, chord position, or chord function. Only harmony—not rhythm and melody—is a factor in the incorrect performances.

61.

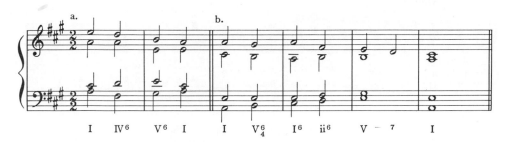

I   IV⁶   V⁶   I   I   V⁶₄   I⁶   ii⁶   V — 7   I

I   vi   ii⁶   V⁷   vi   V⁶   I

62.

Allegro

63.

Allegro

64.

XX

More Rhythmic Counterpoint—Review

Motivic Development (continued)

Imitative Counterpoint (continued)

The initial exercises are intended as a review and continuation of rhythmic patterns more commonly found in instrumental music than in vocal music. The exercises should be performed on two different pitches and two different vowels, and preferably with a third person to serve as conductor and corrector of errors. Each performer, preferably, should cover the other part(s), reading only his own line; however, the exercises may be performed from the complete score, if desired. As always, exchange parts after performing each exercise. Rather than always intoning the exercises, it is good practice to use different instruments, each on a different pitch. If reiterated notes are problematic in certain exercises, alternate between two pitches of a triad (Figure 1–a or b), or between two pitches a step apart (Figure 1–c).

FIGURE 1

PERFORMING

1.

Allegro molto

2.

Andante molto

3.

Presto

4.

Moderato

5.

Alla marcia

6.

7.

8.

9.

LISTENING

Two-Voice Rhythmic Dictation

(*Appendix, p. 292*)

Listen to each exercise completely; then notate both parts. The parts will be played at two different pitch levels and may be played on two different instruments as well; initially the tempo will be established before each exercise, but this procedure should be abandoned after reasonable skill is acquired. Occasionally a structural motive may be imitated between the voices. Three hearings should suffice. Notate the patterns on two different pitch levels, as in the exercises above.

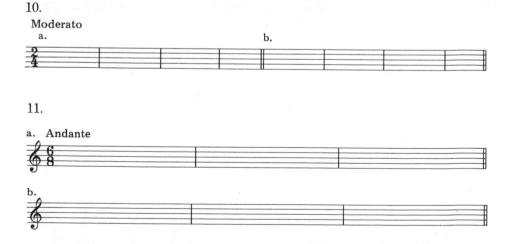

12.

a. **Poco allegro**

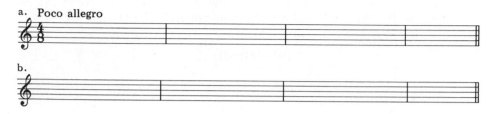

b.

13.

a. **Allegro**

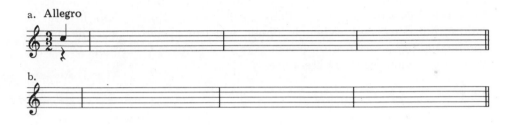

b.

14.

a. **Allegro non troppo**

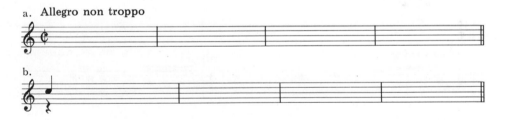

b.

Motivic Development

(Appendix, p. 293)

The following exercises provide further practice in techniques of motivic development, both by listening and by improvisation. Motives may be developed mechanically, by uniform treatment of the entire motive (transposition, augmentation, inversion, etc.) or organically, by working with characteristics unique to a particular motive or part of a motive (adding or deleting portions, altering the rhythm, contour, or intervallic structure, etc.)

15–22. In these exercises, you will be given a motive which will be played twice, followed by a development of that motive. Describe the compositional technique(s) employed in the development of each motive.

PERFORMING

Improvisation

Following are a few basic motives of varying length and character. Sing or play each of them; then develop them using a variety of compositional techniques. If possible, expand each motive into a complete phrase with a logical goal (and cadence). It is important to keep moving—do not interrupt the musical flow by stopping to think about your next move. Spin it out, risk failure, but don't stop. When in doubt, you can always repeat the motive (preferably transposed). Also, invent your own motives to develop, or extract them from various works of literature.

Two-Voice Imitative Counterpoint

The following exercises are a continuation of the procedures introduced in Chapter XVIII. The rhythm will be largely (but not continually) complementary, and your attention will normally shift back and forth between the voices, depending upon which has the more important part (usually indicated by increased motion or by an entrance of a prominent motive). Since the motivic patterns will be similar in both parts, you needn't listen to both lines as if each were an independent melody, but rather to telling intervals between the lines, particularly on the strong beats and at the places where one voice begins to imitate the other. Often, strict imitation will change into non-imitative counterpoint as the composer drives toward a cadence.

LISTENING

Dictation with Notated Signposts

(*Appendix, p. 295*)

Listen closely for motivic imitation, for dissonant intervals and their resolution, for tendency tones, rests, and complementary rhythms. The passages may be repeated, and the longer passages may be broken into shorter segments, if necessary.

25.

26.

27.

Mendelssohn, *Christus*

28.

29.

Bach, "Qui Tollis" (B Minor Mass)

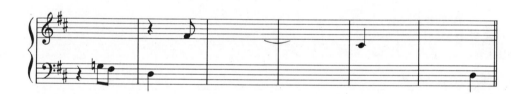

Dictation without Notated Signposts

(*Appendix, p. 296*)

The initial pitch or pitches, but not necessarily the initial rhythmic durations, will be given for each of the exercises. Listen to the complete excerpt, particularly to motivic exchanges, before beginning to write. The key and tempo may be established beforehand, but it is far better practice to begin each exercise "cold."

30.

31.

32.

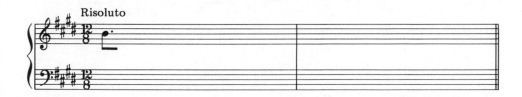

33.

34.

Mendelssohn, *Christus*

35.

Mendelssohn, *Christus*

Error Detection

(*Appendix, p. 298*)

These excerpts from literature will be performed incorrectly, as in previous chapters. Stop the music when you hear an error and correct it immediately, or make a check mark over each passage where an error occurs, later notating the errors directly on the score with a colored pencil. Errors will occur in either the rhythm or the melody, and either singly or in a series. Concentrate on the errors in series first, then on single errors. When an error has been identified and corrected, that segment should be played correctly thereafter. Neither tempo nor key should be established beforehand.

36.

Mendelssohn, Op.19, No.6

37.

Bach, "Et Incarnatus Est" (B Minor Mass)

38.

Brahms, *Requiem* (II)

39.

Bach, Fugue No.2, *The Well-Tempered Clavier*, I

(Moderato)

40.

Bach, "Gloria in Excelsis" (B Minor Mass)

Vivace

41.

Franck, Violin Sonata, IV

Allegretto poco mosso

Piano

42.

Lassus, Motet: *Justus Cor Suum Tradet*

XXI

The Diminished Seventh Chord

Basic Pivot Chord Modulation

Basic Direct Chromatic Modulation

THE DIMINISHED SEVENTH CHORD

Two minor thirds in succession form a tritone (Figure 1a). Three minor thirds form a diminished seventh chord (an interval of a diminished seventh between root and seventh—Figure 1b); and four minor thirds precisely divide an octave into equal segments (Figure 1c). Any combination of minor thirds produces an interesting sonic structure.

FIGURE 1

The diminished seventh chord is one of the most versatile chords in common usage. It is capable of smoothly resolving to or being led into from any chord imaginable, though its normal resolution is to a chord whose root lies a half step above the root of the diminished seventh chord. It is a dominant-functioning chord, resolving to the chord that follows as if to a tonic, and it is capable of being enharmonically respelled in a variety of ways. Because it consists of intervals of a minor third only, one cannot aurally distinguish an inversion from a root position chord; therefore, as with the augmented triad,

113

one should aurally consider the chord to be in root position. However it may actually be spelled, its resolution will determine its theoretical usage. The ambiguity of the chord and its spelling is the reason for its versatility, and is the factor which led to its common use (and not infrequent overuse) by so many composers between 1750 and 1900 and to its continued use by composers of commercial music today.

The diminished seventh chord is constructed of three minor thirds over the leading tone of any given key, and in the normal resolution the diminished seventh interval compresses inward to a fifth. The chord resolves equally well to either a major or a minor tonic chord.

FIGURE 2

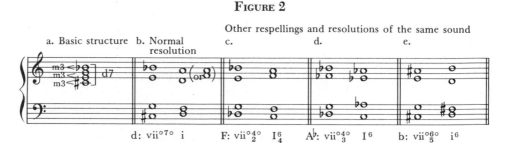

Because all the intervals are identical in size, the diminished seventh chord has a unique sonic quality that identifies it wherever it occurs. Sing the following exercises while focusing on the unique sonic characteristics of the chord. Since the chord sounds the same no matter how it is spelled, it will be referred to henceforth as the o⁷ (diminished seventh) chord without regard for spelling or inversion, and will always be assumed to be in root position.

PERFORMING

3.

4.

5.

Linear Chord Changes

Sing the following exercises, with particular attention to the resolution of each diminished seventh.

6.

7.

8.

9.

LISTENING

Identification of a Diminished Seventh Chord in a Chord Progression

(*Appendix, p. 302*)

10– In each of the following chord progressions, raise your hand every time
12. you hear a diminished seventh chord. On a second hearing, identify the

particular diatonic chord to which each resolves. Preferably, neither key nor meter should be established in advance.

BASIC PIVOT CHORD MODULATION

Modulation (the process of harmonic transition from one tonal center to another) is frequently effected by means of a pivot chord—a chord common to both the original key and the key which is the goal of the modulation. A pivot chord may be likened to the intersection of two streets—common ground shared by both streets. A car may cross the intersection and continue in the same direction, or it may turn the corner and proceed in a new direction. In either instance it passes through the same intersection—only the goal is different.

<small>FIGURE 3</small>

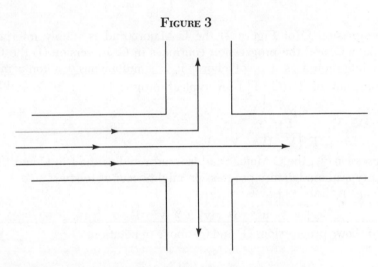

A pivot chord modulation customarily involves three factors:

1) The establishment of the original key
2) The pivot chord itself, which serves one function in the original key and a different function in a new key
3) The establishment (or confirmation) of the new key.

A pitch foreign to the original key will occur in the chord immediately following the pivot chord, and from that point on, the progression is interpreted in the new key.

For example, a C Major chord may serve a variety of functions. It could be the tonic of C Major, the dominant of F Major or minor, the subdominant of G Major, or the submediant of e minor. Figure 4 extends the intersection analogy showing the C Major triad as a pivot chord.

FIGURE 4

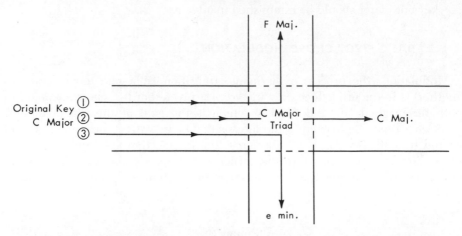

In progression ② (of Figure 4) the C Major triad is simply interpreted as the tonic in C, and the progression continues in C. In version ① the C Major triad is interpreted as a pivot chord—it is simultaneously a tonic in C and the Dominant of F (C I⌐). A typical progression might look like this:
F ⌐V

C: I IV V   I⌐
          F ⌐V IV⁶ V⁶ I

In progression ③, the C Major triad is interpreted as the I in C and the VI in e, and a typical modulatory progression might occur as follows:
C: I vi IV V I⁶⌐
          e ⌐VI⁶ ii°⁶ i⁶ iv i ⁶₄ V⁷ i

Figure 5 shows progressions ① and ③ above in notation.

FIGURE 5

LISTENING

Pivot Chord Exercises

(*Appendix, p. 303*)

13–20. The next eight exercises are all brief progressions involving modulation with a pivot chord. Each of the progressions may be treated in four ways (possibly more, if you are inventive). In order of increasing complexity, the following four procedures are recommended:

(1) As the progression is played, sustain the tonic of the original key shifting to the tonic of the new key after the modulation occurs. *Variant:* Focus on, but do not sing, the tonic of the original key. After the progression is completed, sing the original tonic, then the new tonic. Describe the change of key (e.g., up a major third; C Major to e minor).

(2) As the progression is replayed, raise your hand when you hear the foreign tone(s) in the chord immediately following the pivot. As the progression is replayed again, identify the function of the pivot chord in the original key (e.g., I⁶). If possible, also determine the key to which the modulation occurred and the function of the pivot chord in the new key (e.g., VI⁶).

(3) As the progression is again replayed, write the Roman numerals of the chord progression as it unfolds. It will be useful to preestablish the number of measures in a given progression and to draw the appropriate bar lines on a blank sheet of paper (as in the sample derived from Figure 5, version ①).

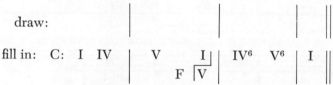

draw:

fill in: C: I   IV | V   I || IV⁶ V⁶ | I ||
                               F |V

(4) As the progression, now familiar, is replayed again, write the soprano and bass lines in dictation. If possible, also notate the tenor and alto parts, but the outer voices remain more essential. Use a separate sheet of score paper.

BASIC DIRECT CHROMATIC MODULATION

Modulation by pivot chord normally produces the smoothest movement from one key to another. Sometimes composers prefer an abrupt or unexpected transition from one key to another, and other times they simply shift from one tonality to another without benefit of modulation. Next to the pivot chord, one of the most common means of modulation from one key to another is by means of a direct chromatic modulation—an unexpected motion into a new key through a dominant-functioning chord in the new key.

Usually the modulation is effected through the leading tone of the new key—a note foreign to the original key. Depending upon the relationship between the two keys, the effect of the modulation may range from agreeably surprising to crude. After the original key is established, the new key is led into through a rising chromatic line in one of the voices. In Figure 6 the melodic progression C-C♯-D produces the modulation from C to D, with the leading tone C♯ being harmonized by the dominant chord of the key of D.

FIGURE 6

LISTENING

(Appendix, p. 306)

21– Follow the four procedures described for performing the exercises
27. dealing with pivot chord modulation (exercises 13–20 above). Procedure two should be adjusted slightly as follows: Raise your hand when you

hear the direct chromatic motion which produces the modulation. As the exercise is replayed, identify the voice in which the chromatic motion occurs and the function of the chord immediately preceding the chromatic leading tone.

Melodic motion through the leading tone of a new key is by far the most common means of direct modulation, but two other means are also used occasionally. In all instances the new key is entered through dominant harmony, however.

A new key may also be approached by *descent* through the chord seventh of a V⁷ or diminished seventh chord, or by a common tone relationship with some member of a dominant-functioning chord in the new key. Frequently these techniques are used in combination with each other or with the more common *ascending* approach through the leading tone. The effect of the chromatic modulation is dependent upon both the relationship between the keys and the voice leading, and may range from imperceptibly smooth through pleasantly surprising to wrenchingly abrupt. Figure 7 shows direct modulation by means of: (a) descent through the chord seventh, (b) common tone relationship, and (c) a combination of both techniques.

FIGURE 7

LISTENING

(Appendix, p. 307)

28– Follow the same procedures as before, with the following modification of
31.   procedure 2: Raise your hand when you hear the chromatic motion away
from the original key. As the progression is replayed, determine whether
the modulation is accomplished through a descending seventh, leading
tone, common tone, or a combination of means. Try also to determine in
which voice(s) the modulatory motion occurs. Direct chromatic modulation
can be very complex. Therefore don't be discouraged if you cannot hear all
the factors operating at any given time. It is more important to recognize
when it occurs then *how* it occurs, and to hear the relationship between
the two tonalities.

More Four-Voice Dictation

(Appendix, p. 308)

Write the appropriate chord numerals below the bass clef as well as
notating the soprano and bass voices. Certain information is occasionally
given, especially for unexpected chords. The blanks indicate the number
of chord changes in each measure. At least one modulation occurs in each
exercise, and you should fully indicate the pivot chord (occurring directly
before the first chord with functional chromaticism) or, if there is no common
chord, the point where the direct modulation occurs (directly on the chord
with functional chromaticism, if the previous chord is not common to both
keys).

As before, the object of these exercises is to correlate the chord function
(Roman numerals) with the melodic lines in the soprano and bass. If possible,
divide your attention between the melodic and harmonic aspects, listening to
both simultaneously. If this is too difficult, listen to the counterpoint first,
later inferring the chords from your melodic observations. At any given
moment, either the melodic or the harmonic factor may predominate, and
your attention will be guided in such instances. It is excellent practice, as
always, to write the alto and tenor lines as well, but the outside lines still
predominate. It may be impractical to attempt writing the inner voices in
certain styles (melody with moving accompaniment, instrumentally conceived
piano sonata, etc.).

The tonality will be established before each exercise in a new key, and the
exercises will be repeated as necessity demands.

32.

a.

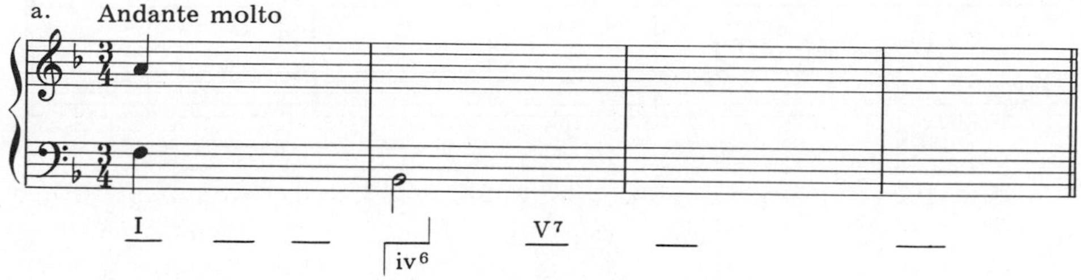
Andante molto
I
iv6
V7

b.

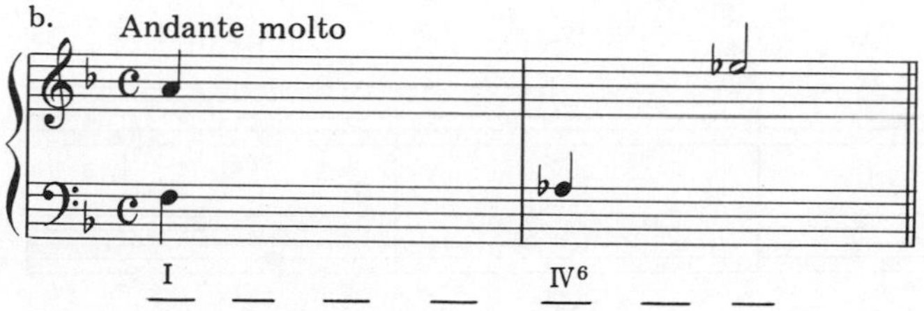
Andante molto
I
IV6

33.

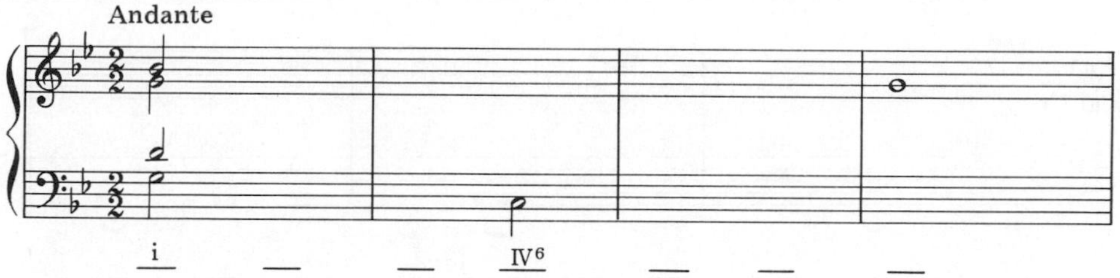
Andante
i
IV6

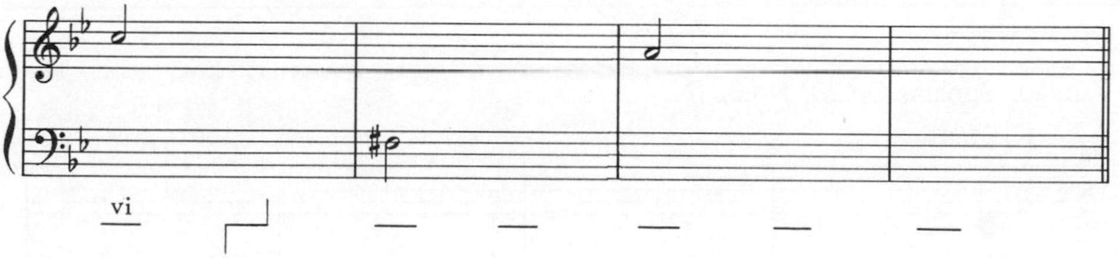
vi

34.

Mendelssohn, *Christus*

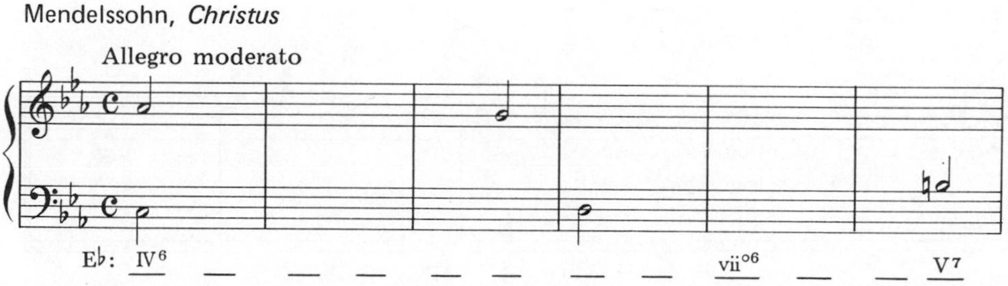
Allegro moderato
E♭: IV6
vii°6
V7

iii   ii$^6_5$

35.

Bach, Chorale No.160

(Moderato)

V iii   iii

ii

36.

Kuhlau, Sonata, Op.20, No.3, II

Larghetto

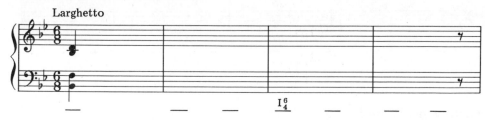

I$^6_4$

i^6

37.

Error Detection with a Given Chord Series

(*Appendix, p. 311*)

Before beginning each series below, you are to imagine the sound of each progression, some chords of which will be played incorrectly. On the first hearing, listen to the complete passage, noting where the errors occur. On subsequent hearings, stop the music and correct the errors as they occur. Unlike earlier chapters, where the errors occurred singly or occasionally in a short series, in these exercises there are some longer series of errors, including modulations through the wrong pivot chord or to the wrong key. Nonharmonic tones sometimes occur as well, depending upon the exercise. The initial exercises are in block chords; later exercises contain more rhythmic variety. The key, but not necessarily the tempo, will be established beforehand.

38.

Moderato

Eb: $\frac{2}{2}$ I   vi | V$\frac{4}{3}$ i | VII| V^7 | I   ‖
c   Eb| V

39.

Moderato

C: $\frac{2}{2}$ I   V^6 | I^6 V$\frac{6}{5}$ | I   V^7 | I   ‖
Eb

40.

Moderato

d: $\frac{2}{2}$ i   o^7 | i^6 V$\frac{4}{3}$ | I^6 o^7 | I   o^7 | i   V^7 | i   ‖
c   d

41.

Andante

c#: $\frac{3}{4}$ i   iv | V   i   iv^6| V$\frac{6}{5}$ I^6 V | I   ‖
A| vi^6

42.

Mendelssohn

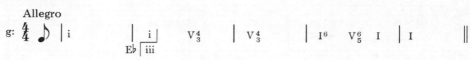

43.

Klengel

Andante molto

F: $\frac{6}{8}$ I | V$^4_3$ | V^2 V^6 | I $\lfloor$o^7 | i$^6_4$ | $\lfloor$o^7 V^7 V^2 | i^6 ii^{o6} V^7 | i ‖
g   c

44.

Allegro moderato

B: $\frac{12}{8}$ I V$^6_5$ I V^7 | vi ii$^6_4$ vi | V$^6_5$ | I IV$^6_4$ I | IV | I$^6_4$ V I ‖
F♯   B | I

Error Detection from Score

(Appendix, p. 313)

Each of the following excerpts is correctly notated but will be performed incorrectly. Stop the music when you hear an error, and correct the performer. Allow a reasonable segment to be played before stopping the flow of the music, especially if an error occurs immediately. It is always excellent practice to mark the errors directly on the score, notating them with a colored pencil. Key and tempo should *not* be established before each excerpt.

45.

Kuhlau, Sonatina, Op.55, No.2, II

46.

Chopin, Mazurka, Op.68, No.3

47.

Bach, Sarabande (French Suite I)

48.

Beethoven, Sonata, Op.49, No.1, I

49.

Mozart, Sonata, K.280, I

50.

Beethoven, Sonata, Op.14, No.1, I

51.

Beethoven, Sonata, Op.13, I

XXII

Irregular Divisions of the Beat More Syncopation; Instrumentally-Conceived Melody; Broader Aspects of Rhythm; Instrumentally-Conceived Counterpoint

IRREGULAR DIVISIONS OF THE BEAT

Several times you have encountered rhythmic patterns in previous chapters in which the beats are momentarily *not* divided into normal symmetrical portions, but into irregular portions instead. Such irregular division has been used throughout the history of music, particularly in instrumental music, and has become progressively more common up to the present time.

The common meters that normally show a duple division may also be divided into 3, 5, 6, 7, etc., instead of two or multiples thereof. Division into 3 and 5 are by far the most frequently encountered irregular divisions and will be the only divisions systematically treated in this chapter. All irregular divisions of *duply-divided* note values (o, 𝅗𝅥, ♩, ♪, 𝅘𝅥𝅯, 𝅘𝅥𝅰 etc.) contain *more* notes than the normal division.

FIGURE 1

PERFORMING

Intone the following exercises on a neutral vowel, paying scrupulous attention to the difference between rhythmic figures that sound similar, but are subtly different (e.g., ♩♪♪ and ♪♪♩, or ♩. ♪ and ♩³♩).

Various Tempi. Note: Notation is similar in quadruple meters.

1.

a.

b.

c.

2.

3.

4.

5.

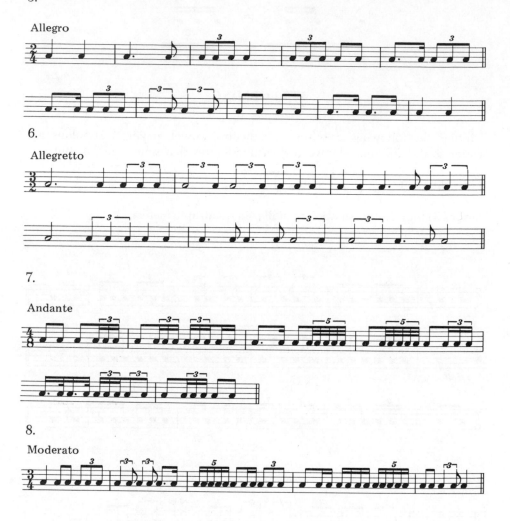

6.

7.

8.

In contrast, irregular divisions of *triply-divided* note values (♩., ♪., ♪., etc.) contain *fewer* notes than the normal division. Division into two or four are the most common irregular groupings and will be treated in this chapter. Other divisions are also possible, though rare, and would be handled similarly.

FIGURE 2

9.

At various tempi

10.

11.

Allegretto

12.

Moderato

13.

14.

LISTENING

Recognition of Irregular Divisions

(Appendix, p. 319)

As the following melodies are played, raise your hand whenever you hear an irregular division of the beat. On subsequent hearings, be prepared to identify the nature of each irregularity, and be able to notate the rhythms. Neither key nor tempo will be established, though the meter is given for the first few exercises.

15. Allegro moderato $\frac{6}{16}$

16. Allegro C

17. Flowing $\frac{3}{2}$

18. Andante con moto $\frac{4}{8}$

19. Adagio cantabile $\frac{2}{4}$ Beethoven

20. Allegro molto vivace $\frac{4}{4}$ Tchaikovsky

21. Andantino $\frac{3}{4}$ Fauré

22. Andantino $\frac{6}{8}$ Schumann

MORE SYNCOPATION

Syncopation was introduced early in this book and has appeared from time to time in excerpts throughout the text. The next few exercises contain a concentration of syncopation and are intended to be intoned, sung, or played as a means of review. Remember that syncopation is the dislocation of an expected accent pattern by either the addition or omission of an accent. The underlying beat must be continually maintained in the mind's ear, no matter how disruptive the syncopation. The more successfully you can maintain the underlying metric pulse, the keener your perception of the syncopation. Whenever possible, conduct the patterns as you perform them.

PERFORMING

28.

Vivaldi, Concerto Grosso Op.3, No.11, 3rd mvt.

29.

Schumann, Piano Sonata, No.2, Op.22, 1st mvt.

30.

J.S.Bach, Brandenburg Concerto No.2, 1st mvt.

31. Take a melody you have recently studied or with which you are familiar and explore ways of inserting syncopation into your performance of it in order to create more excitement. The value of the exercise lies in the doing of the improvisation itself, not necessarily in the results of your efforts. If the piece remains better in its original form even after all your efforts to enliven it, this is a tribute to the original composer's skill as a musical craftsman.

32. Invent brief melodic lines exhibiting various aspects of syncopation. Some

may be for instruments, others for voice; some triadic, some scalar; some employing syncopation by addition, others by omission; some with rests, others continuous; some with normal divisions of the beats, others irregular; and most, no doubt, would employ a combination of means. Once you begin an improvisation, don't hesitate for any reason. Let your innate musical sense range ahead of your rational and critical faculties, and maintain the pulse at all times.

Hemiola

One of the most effective and sophisticated rhythmic techniques commonly employed by composers from the Middle Ages to the present is the device of *hemiola* (from a Greek word meaning the ratio of 1½ to 1 [or 3 to 2])—the shifting of a rhythmic pattern from three beats to two, or from two beats to three. The device is most commonly found in triple meter wherein a passage sounds as if written in duple meter as a result of a consistent shift of musical accents (rhythm, contour, articulation, etc.).

FIGURE 3: HEMIOLA

Hemiola is basically a consistent syncopation involving an exchange between two and three. More often than not, hemiola will occur near the end of a passage and often, in choral music especially, serves to brake the rhythmic flow prior to a cadence. Intone the initial exercises and sing, if possible, or play, the following characteristic examples from musical literature.

PERFORMING

33.

Moderato

34.

Allegro non troppo

35.

Allegro

36.

Andante

37.

Mozart, Symphony, No.40, 3rd mvt.

Allegretto

38.

Brahms, Symphony No.2, 1st mvt.

Allegro non troppo

39.

Tchaikovsky, *Nutcracker* Suite, Op.71a, "Waltz of the Flowers"

Con anima

40.

Beethoven, Cello Sonata No.3, Op.69, 4th mvt.

Allegro vivace

41.

Brahms, *German Requiem,* 3rd mvt.

Andante moderato

The term "hemiola" is sometimes extended to include the simultaneous sounding of three against two, as is found so frequently in piano literature. Actually, three against two is only one illustration of polyrhythm (though no doubt the most predominant), of which numerous other numerical combinations are possible (five against four, four against three, etc.) Single-line performers should not encounter much difficulty with three against two, since they will contend with only one division of the beat, but pianists particularly must practice the rhythms in combination, a study in coordination outside the bounds of this text. A few exercises involving the simultaneous combination of three and two are given below, to be performed in counterpoint on two different vowels and on two different pitches. In performing the exercise, cover the opposite part and exchange parts when each exercise is completed.

PERFORMING

42.

Allegro moderato

43.

Allegretto

44.

Andante

LISTENING

Error Detection—Syncopation, Hemiola, Irregular Divisions

(*Appendix, p. 320*)

The following passages will be performed with rhythmic errors. On the first hearing, make a check mark over (or under) the errors you detect, and on a subsequent hearing, stop the music and correct each error (or set of errors) as it occurs. Once an error is detected and corrected, it should henceforth be performed correctly.

45.

Allegro non troppo

46.

Vivace (in one)

47.

Adagio

48.

Moderato

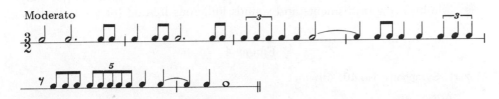

49.

Adagio

50.

Allegro

51.

Tempo di valse

INSTRUMENTALLY-CONCEIVED MELODY

Most people perceive melody as a singable line, one that flows logically, is easily remembered, and is readily negotiable by the human voice. Such melodies also are usually rather limited in range and are uncomplicated rhythmically, and would make an impressive effect played by a variety of instruments as well as the human voice. Such melodies are considered to be, not surprisingly, *vocally-conceived*.

In contrast, the Violin I line of the opening of the fourth movement of Mozart's Symphony No. 40, clearly the primary focus of attention, is only playable by a few instruments and sounds ludicrous if sung (or attempted).

Figure 4

Mozart, Symphony No.40, 4th mvt.

Spanning more than two octaves, the line exhibits rhythmic, dynamic, and articulation contrasts, and contains a succession of intervals too difficult for the human voice to sing in tempo. It is idiomatically written for the violin and hence is *instrumentally-conceived*. While vocally-conceived melody is *universal*, capable of being sung or played by a wide variety of instruments, instrumentally-conceived melody is *idiomatic*, clearly better suited for the instrument for which it was written than for others, and specifically not intended for the human voice.

In essence, instrumentally-conceived melody is any that is not readily singable, and innumerable factors can be used individually or in combination to make a line non-vocal. Melodically, instrumentally-conceived melodies tend to involve rapid scale passages or broken chords, and often feature wide leaps of register. They often span a considerable range, and exhibit marked contrasts of articulations and rhythmic patterns, often containing syncopations and irregular divisions of beats as previously studied in this chapter. They also often employ figural patterns unique to the given instrument (e.g., two-octave broken chord accompaniment pattern for piano, arpeggiation across three or four strings for string instruments, triple tonguing for brass and wind instruments, etc.).

Instrumentally-conceived melodies have been encountered frequently in this book and are part of the basic listening background of every musician. Following are a few melodies that will be played incorrectly, in which you are to correct the errors according to the familiar process encountered in previous chapters.

LISTENING

Error Detection in a Melodic Context

(*Appendix, p. 323*)

52.

Beethoven, Sonata, Op.2, No.2, 1st mvt.

53.

Haydn, Symphony No.92 *(Oxford)*, 1st mvt.

54.

Beethoven, Sonata, Op.2, No.1

55.

56.

Brahms, Cello Sonata, Op.38, 3rd mvt.

PERFORMING

57. Improvise some instrumentally-conceived melodies on any instrument with which you are comfortable, using the melodies above or below as models. Initially you might wish to stress only one instrumental factor (wide leaps, syncopation, rapid scale passages, etc.), later combining these elements into longer or more sophisticated lines.

LISTENING

Analytical Listening

(*Appendix, p. 325*)

Listen to each of the following excerpts; then describe the way in which the melody is constructed to achieve the unique effect of the passage. In other words, what happens? How is the excerpt organized? What musical factors are being utilized? Are they used individually or in combination? Consider such factors as contour, rhythm, phrasing, tendency tones, dynamics, etc. Often one (or two) of these factors will predominate as the basic organizing principle, as in Figure 5.

FIGURE 5

Comment: A reiterated rhythmic pattern (short-long) is used consistently to form two phrases, the antecedent ending on the dominant and the consequent cadencing on the tonic. The accented beats form a steadily ascending major scale.

Describe the following excerpts similarly. The meter, tempo, number of measures, and composer and composition are given to you.

58.

From Beethoven, Sonata, Op.7, I

Allegro molto e con brio

59.

Schumann, Sonata No.2, Op.22, I

Presto (Allegro)

60.

Beethoven, Sonata, Op.10, No.1, Finale

Prestissimo

61.

Mozart, Serenade K.525, "Eine kleine Nachtmusik"

Allegro

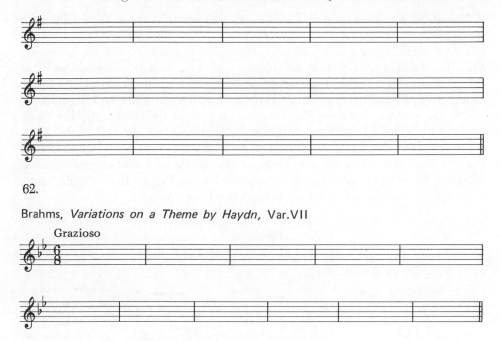

62.

Brahms, *Variations on a Theme by Haydn,* Var.VII

BROADER ASPECTS OF RHYTHM

Rhythm is perhaps the single most important element in all musical organization—even more important than pitch organization. There are many compositions in which melodic interest is minimal, in which, for instance, chord successions, shifting textures, or strikingly contrasting dynamic levels are more important, at least in certain passages. All these musical elements must be organized in time, however—time is the element central to music of all eras, all styles, and all cultures.

Attention has been focused to date on relatively small units of time—on the beat and its divisions and subdivisions, and on characteristic combinations of various durations (source patterns). Rhythm is an important organizing factor at broader levels as well, contributing significantly to the aural perception of musical flow into larger units of one or two measures, semi-phrases, phrases, periods, and large sections. Rhythm thus helps delineate form.

Since all musical elements exist in time, it follows that all elements may be organized rhythmically and that composers may deliberately manipulate the rate or kind of change in these elements to produce a pattern in time. For example, in certain compositions there may be a persistent alteration between high winds and low strings, producing a perceptible patterned registral rhythm (high-low) and timbral rhythm (wind-strings). Beethoven, for example, made frequent use of such patterns. Most pieces exhibit a characteristic harmonic rhythm (rate of change from one chord to another), which may be altered deliberately at the opening of a new section to create contrast, or which may be deliberately changed for a specific purpose (as, for instance, the braking effect of hemiola prior to a cadence). Harmonic rhythm, especially, is important in establishing the style or character of a particular composition. The temporal organization of all these elements should be considered as you listen to any piece of music, along with the obvious matters of pitch and duration.

For the present, consider the broader aspects of durational rhythm as it works with melody to produce larger units of perception. Several of the compositions previously heard in Exercises 58–62 above are obviously divided into perceptible aural units on the basis of the rhythmic-melodic organization. Number 60, for example, which appears below as Figure 6, is divided into several short units which combine to form two larger phrases.

FIGURE 6

Beethoven, Sonata Op.10, No.1

Commentary: A one-measure rhythmic-melodic motive is stated, then immediately repeated with a slight interval expansion. Another repetition with a larger interval expansion is extended for an additional measure, finally cadencing on an implied dominant. The motive is transposed down (to the dominant) and repeated and expanded as before, and a new two-measure semi-phrase of continuous eighth-note motion outlining a diminished seventh chord leads to a melodic climax and a cadence on the tonic. In retrospect, the first half of the passage is heard as an antecedent phrase, and the last half as a consequent phrase.

Analytical Listening

(*Appendix, p. 327*)

63– Listen to the following passages and describe their organization, with
68. special attention to the relationship between rhythm and melody as they combine to form large patterns. One of the patterns frequently encountered will be two short units followed by a single matching (or completing) unit twice as long.

Instrumentally-Conceived Counterpoint—Error Detection
(*Appendix, p. 329*)

Most of the counterpoint encountered previously has been vocally-conceived, with a few exceptions. Following are some excerpts from literature which are more instrumentally-conceived, and are thus somewhat more intricate. All are notated correctly but will be performed with errors. Stop the music when you hear an error and correct it immediately, or make a check mark over each passage where an error occurs, later notating the errors directly on the score with a colored pencil. Concentrate on the errors in a series first, then on isolated errors. When an error has been identified and corrected, that segment should be played correctly thereafter. Neither key nor tempo should be established beforehand.

69.

Bach, Invention XIII

(Allegro)

70.

Bach, Invention XIV

(Andante con moto)

71.

Mozart, Symphony No.41, IV

72.

Bach, Invention VI

XXIII

Summary Review:

Rhythm, Melody, Counterpoint

Analytical Listening

These final two chapters are designed as an overview of the material and procedures of all the previous chapters, and nothing specifically new will be introduced in them. They are intended as a general, not an exhaustive, review, and will summarize material in an order of increasing complexity, similar to the progression from chapter to chapter which is the basic format of these two volumes. Naturally more emphasis will be placed on the more complex material of the later chapters than on the more basic material of the initial chapters.

Use the review diagnostically; when problems are encountered with a certain musical procedure, return to the chapter or chapters in which that procedure is presented and *carefully, methodically,* and *thoughtfully* review and practice the contents of the chapter. It is human nature to prefer to do those things that come naturally to you and which require the least effort, and to slight those things that are unfamiliar, uncomfortable, or which require substantial effort. Resist the temptation to practice only the comfortable. Most musicians encounter more difficulty with certain areas of ear training than with others and may always find those areas more vexing to deal with than those which come naturally. Don't be discouraged if you don't manage to *eliminate* a problem. What is important is that with practice and patience you can improve. You are unlikely ever to be a *perfect* musician; you can always, however, be a better musician.

RHYTHM

In general, rhythm tends to be fundamentally organized in basic source patterns that reflect and support the prevailing meter, wherein agogic accents usually occur on the strong beats, particularly on the downbeat.

FIGURE 1: BASIC SOURCE PATTERNS

These patterns may be considered the norm, the foundation upon which variants are built.

Because these source patterns support the meter so strongly, their very regularity and predictability can become tiresome if used too long. Syncopation, or disruption of the regular accent pattern, is one of the primary means of achieving rhythmic variety, and occurs when an accent is either added or omitted. Syncopation, to be effective, must be felt in relation to the underlying metric pattern. Further variety can be achieved by more complex subdivisions of the beat and by irregular divisions of the beat (into odd numbers if the beat is a quarter, half, or eighth, or into even numbers if the beat is a dotted note). Rhythm patterns, in conjunction with melody, operate at broader levels than the beat or its divisions, shaping music into larger units of perception (one measure or more, semiphrase, phrase, period, etc.) which determine the form of the piece. Hemiola also creates rhythmic variety by introducing metric ambiguity—two within a triple meter or three within a duple meter.

Perform these review exercises using the standard procedures. The exercises become progressively more complex, beginning with the basic source patterns. With the simpler exercises, it is excellent practice to tap or clap them, since that involves a mechanical action akin to playing an instrument. Exercises should also be intoned, especially those involving syncopation, since by intoning, an oral distinction can be made between a tie and a rest. Whenever possible, and as often as possible, conduct the beat pattern as the exercise is performed. Rhythm should always be felt relative to a constant pulse, especially in response to a physical gesture.

PERFORMING

Single Line

Tempi are moderately fast, unless otherwise indicated.

1.

2.

3.

4.

5.

6.

Moderato molto

7.

8.

9.

Two-Voice Counterpoint

Use different instruments, different pitches, different vowels, etc. For maximum benefit, cover the other line(s), reading only the line you are performing. Always exchange parts.

10.

11.

12.

13.

Allegro

14.

Moderato

15.

Adagio

16.

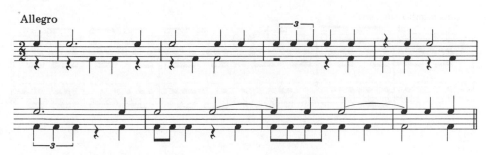

Three-Voice Counterpoint

17.

18.

19.

20.

Poco adagio (in two)

21.

Grazioso

Rhythmic Improvisation

22. Expand each of the following rhythmic statements into a complete phrase, ending with a logical rhythmic cadence.

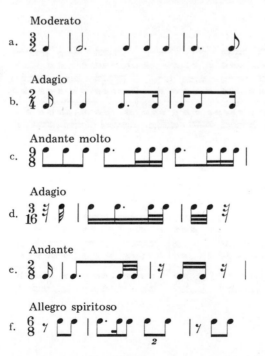

a. Moderato

b. Adagio

c. Andante molto

d. Adagio

e. Andante

f. Allegro spiritoso

23. With three or more people, take string quartets, sonatas, symphonies, or other instrumental compositions; seek out a fairly active section from the middle of a movement and intone the rhythm, using different pitches, instruments, or vowels for each of the various lines.

LISTENING

Recognition of Specific Factors
(Appendix, p. 334)

Raise your hand when (or if) you hear the factor specified before each exercise. If you make an error, listen to that segment performed *slowly;* then *slowly* intone the passage yourself, followed by the correct patterns.

24.

Moderato

25.

Allegro

26.

Larghetto

27.

Allegro moderato

28.

Marcato

29.

Moderato

Distinguishing Between Similar Patterns

In the following exercises, two slightly different versions of a similar rhythmic pattern are given. Identify which of the two versions is played. The performer may choose either pattern; there is no particular "correct" version. It is better practice to begin the exercises "cold," without establishing the tempo beforehand.

30.

Allegro

31.

Andante

32.

Adagio

33.

Allegro marziale

34.

Andante con moto

35.

Grazioso

36.

Adagio non troppo

37.

Allegro

Dictation

(*Appendix, p. 335*)

Follow standard procedures. All two-voice dictation should, of course, be performed at two different pitches or on two different vowels. The less repetition, the more challenging the exercise.

38.

Andante

39.

Allegretto

40.

Allegro

41.

Poco adagio

42.

Andante con moto

43.

Grazioso

44.

Allegro molto

45.

Moderato

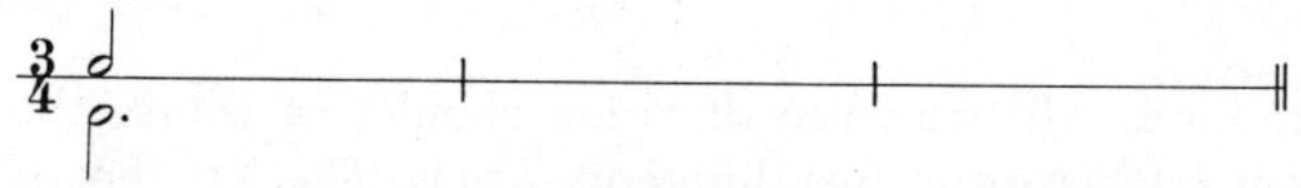

46.

Moderato

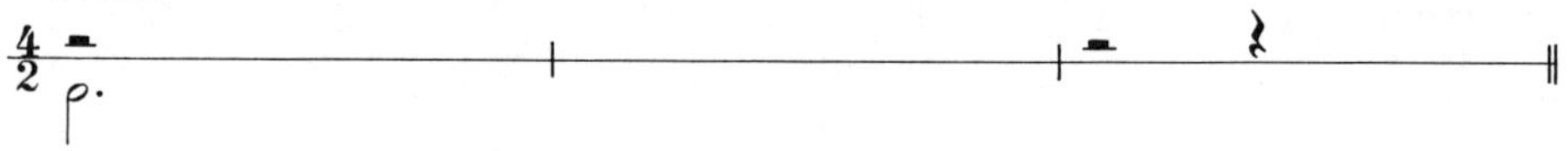

47.

Alla marcia

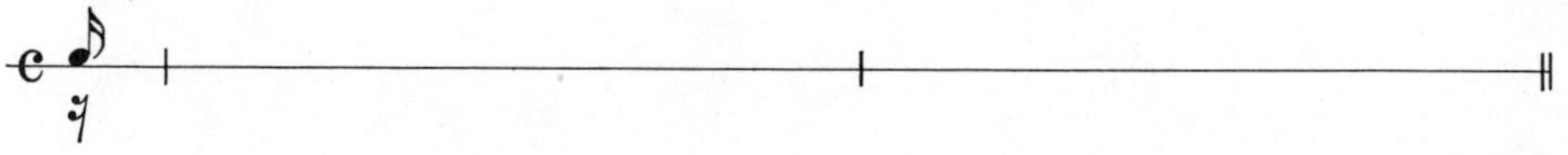

48.

Moderato

Error Detection

(Appendix, p. 337)

As errors occur in the following patterns, either stop the music or suggest corrections, or make a check mark over the errors, later notating the rhythm as it was incorrectly performed.

49.

Allegretto

50.

Andante

51.

Allegro moderato

52.

Poco andante

53.

Allegro

54.

Moderato

55.

Grazioso

56.

Poco adagio

57.

Allegro non troppo

58.

Poco allegro

MELODY

The two most important aspects of melody are the rhythm and the pitch organization. Pitches in tonal music are regarded as either relatively active or relatively stable, depending upon their location within the scale structure of the prevailing key. It is unrealistic to speak in absolute terms, but generally the pitches of the tonic triad (1, 3, and 5) are relatively stable in all keys, while the others are more active in varying degrees. Those active pitches a half step away from a stable pitch show a stronger tendency to resolve by half step than those a whole step apart.

In a major key the tendency tones and their resolutions are 7–8 and 4–3. Various forms of the minor mode are used, often in alternation, all of which have slightly different characteristics. In general, the strong leading tone tendency (7–8) is maintained in most minor contexts, and the half step tendency 6–5 appears more often than not. The characteristic tone of the minor third is common to all forms of the minor mode—in fact, the lower pentachord is identical in all forms of the minor scale; only the upper tetrachord varies.

Tendency tones tend to push strongly onward to their note of resolution; stable tones are usually structurally important, frequently occurring on strong beats and generally reinforcing the meter. Other active tones often serve as connectors, as in the melodic progression 1-2-3, where 2 connects stable tones 1 and 3. It is important to hear the distinction between stable and active tones —and particularly to recognize stable tones 1 and 5 when they appear prominently—and to hear the leading tone resolution in all keys, the 4-3 tendency in major, and the 6-5 in minor modes.

Melody tends to move primarily in conjunct motion, with occasional telling skips, or in patterns outlining important triads within the key—particularly the tonic and dominant chords. Not all melodic pitches are equal in importance. Some are structural—outlining, undergirding, and defining the melody, which would be different in character were the structural pitches arranged differently —and others are decorative—modifying, connecting, and encircling the basic structural pitches.

The most common decorative pitches are the basic nonharmonic tone patterns. The neighboring tone and passing tone, for instance, tend to illuminate the more important role of the surrounding structural tones, and the appoggiatura and suspension lean heavily on the harmonic tones that follow. Usually structural tones occur on strong beats, while less important nonharmonic tones occur on offbeats, with the striking exception of the appoggiatura and suspension, which are strong dissonances occurring on the beat. Listen especially for structurally important pitches that occur regularly on strong beats, and which over a larger span (of two or more measures) create a perceptible pitch pattern (such as a scale line) from strong beat to strong beat.

Most melodies, especially vocally-conceived, will tend to be framed within a set of consistent structural pitch boundaries (usually the lowest and highest structural pitch, with another focal structural pitch somewhere in between).

Many melodies will be constructed from brief motives—germinal rhythm-pitch patterns that possess a distinctive identity and are capable of being transformed to reveal more musical implications than were immediately apparent when the motives first appeared. In motivic development, some aspect of the original motive must be maintained (rhythm, intervallic organization, or contour), while the remainder may be varied. As soon as perceptible contact with the original motive is lost, the aural validity of motivic development is questionable.

Though much melody is singable, or readily transferable from one instrument to another, some melody is idiomatically written for a particular instrument, exhibiting a sweep of range, a succession of intervals, or a rhythmic structure clearly not easily sung by the human voice. Instrumentally-conceived melody of this sort may well be the primary line in focus at any given moment and is every bit as worthy of being regarded as "melody" as the more easily understood vocally-conceived melody.

To most listeners, melody is the obvious surface of music, and carries a large proportion of the immediate musical meaning. One can be easily swept along by melody—perhaps in itself one characteristic of a successful melody—but some perceptive discernment of the means which make a given melody move will lead to a deeper and fuller musical understanding.

PERFORMING

Sing these melodies on a neutral vowel, always with an awareness of the interrelationship of musical factors reviewed above—active and stable tones, nonharmonic tones, framing, motivic development, etc. Two variations in performance should be explored also. (1) Stop singing aloud, continue to read silently, and then sing again later (perhaps at a given signal). (2) Establish the tonic and begin conducting, but do not sing until later (again, perhaps at a given signal).

59.

60.

61.

62.

63.

64.

Brahms, *Verrat*

65.

Mozart, *An Chloe*

66. Improvise simple melodies, each leading to a satisfying conclusion, within the following guidelines:

    a. Lower pentachord only—minor key

    b. Upper tetrachord only—melodic minor

    c. Scalar motion only—natural minor scale

    d. Scalar motion only—major

    e. Emphasizing intervals of major third and perfect fourth

    f. Emphasizing intervals of minor sixth and tritone

    g. Emphasizing interval of minor second with dotted rhythm

    h. Emphasizing syncopation

67. Improvise melodic continuations of the following initial motives, leading, as always, to a satisfying cadence.

68. Invent your own melodies, either self-imposing restrictions as in 66 above, spinning out a melodic motive as in 67 above, or simply improvising freely. It is best to establish a key and tempo, then plunge in without preplanning. Risk failure, but keep moving.

LISTENING

Error Detection

(*Appendix, p. 339*)

On the first hearing, mark those places where errors occur, stopping the music and correcting them on subsequent hearings. Use a colored pencil if you notate the errors directly on the music.

69.

Mendelssohn, "Lost Happiness," Op.38, No.2

70.

Brahms, Intermezzo, Op.118, No.2

71.

Mendelssohn, "The Return," Op.85, No.5

72.

Beethoven, Sonata, Op.14, No.2, I

73.

Beethoven, Sonata, Op.22, IV

74.

Franck, Sonata for Violin and Piano, I

75.

Chopin, Ballade, No.1, Op.23

Dictation with Guideposts

(*Appendix, p. 343*)

Several of the following exercises have a given bass line, over which you are to notate the melodic line. Others show key pitches or longer melodic fragments as an aid to orientation within the melodic line. Write the complete melodic line. The exercises should not be repeated frequently.

76.

Clementi, Sonatina, Op.36, No.4, II

77.

Clementi, Sonatina, Op.36, No.2, III

I V⁶ I V⁶ I V⁶ I V⁶

78.

Mendelssohn, "The Wanderer," Op.30, No.4

V⁶ i iv⁶ V

V⁶ i i⁶₄ V i
f♯ | iv

79.

Mendelssohn, "Contemplation," Op.30, No.1

80.

Schumann, Piano Concerto, Op.54, III

Dictation without Guideposts

(*Appendix, p. 344*)

Notate the following melodic lines. The key and meter may be established beforehand, but there should be a minimum of repetition. As the melodies become progressively longer, listen for larger units of organization—repetition or transposition of motives, a consistent pitch pattern, connecting strong beats, etc.

81.

82.

83.

84.

85.

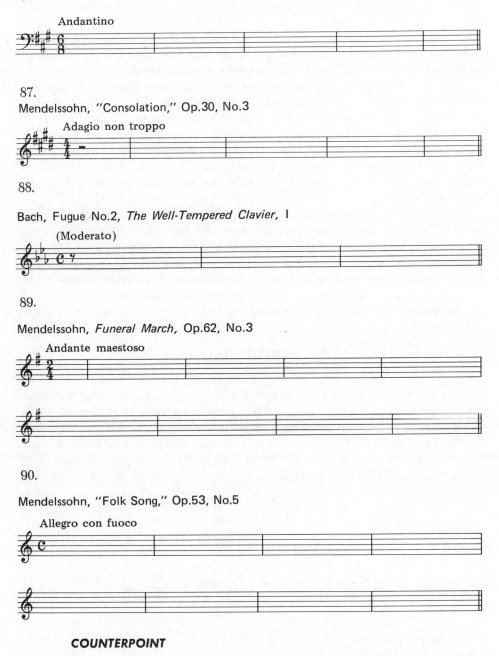

86.

Andantino

87.

Mendelssohn, "Consolation," Op.30, No.3

Adagio non troppo

88.

Bach, Fugue No.2, *The Well-Tempered Clavier,* I

(Moderato)

89.

Mendelssohn, *Funeral March,* Op.62, No.3

Andante maestoso

90.

Mendelssohn, "Folk Song," Op.53, No.5

Allegro con fuoco

COUNTERPOINT

Almost all music in Western civilization exhibits certain attributes of counterpoint—to some extent there is a "give-and-take" relationship between the highest and lowest lines of all multi-voiced music, and, to a less apparent extent, among the other lines as well. Only if the lines are perceived as equal (or approximately equal) participating partners is the texture regarded as contrapuntal.

If the lines are similar in character, exchanging common motives, the counterpoint is regarded as imitative; if the lines are dissimilar in character, independent of one another, the counterpoint is nonimitative.

With all counterpoint, the ear must follow the different lines simultaneously, which requires considerably more effort than following only the primary line in a homophonic context. One's focus of attention shifts back and forth from line to line, rather in a diagonal manner, usually centering on the newest or most striking sonic event of the moment—a new entrance of a motive, a fresh rhythmic pattern, a telling interval, etc. One must learn not just to follow the event of the moment, but to *relate* that event to the rest of the ongoing texture.

Most counterpoint is rhythmically complementary—when one voice moves, another is stable. Dissonance is usually carefully controlled. The strong beats are often consonant and stable, particularly at important structural points (cadences, etc), with incidental nonharmonic activity between beats. An important and common reversal of this condition occurs in a context emphasizing suspensions or appoggiature. In such a context the dissonance is emphasized on the strong beats, with the consonant resolutions occurring on weaker parts of the measure.

PERFORMING

As a prelude to various contrapuntal listening problems, sing the next few exercises on a neutral vowel with a partner, paying particular attention to dissonance-resolution patterns, complementary rhythm, striking intervals or rhythmic patterns, tendency tones, motivic exchanges, and other similar factors which constitute the contrapuntal organization of the exercises. Exchange parts and perform them again.

91.

92.

93.

Moderato

94.

Poco allegro

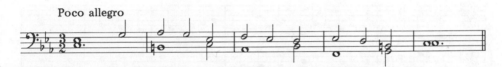

95.

Allegretto

96.

Allegro non troppo

97.

Allegro

98.

Allegro moderato

99.

Bach, "Qui Tollis" (B Minor Mass)

100.

Bach, "Et in Unum Dominum" (B Minor Mass)

LISTENING

Dictation with Notated Signposts

(*Appendix, p. 346*)

As before, listen closely for motivic relationships between the lines, for dissonant intervals and their resolution, for tendency tones, rests, and complementary rhythms. Longer passages may be broken into shorter segments if necessary, but repetition of the passages should be kept to a minimum.

101.

105.

Mendelssohn, Fugue, Op.35

Con moto ma sostenuto

106.

Beethoven, Quartet, Op.18, No.2, IV

107.

Beethoven, Quartet, Op.59, No.3, II

Andante con moto

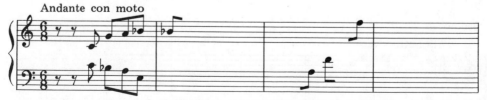

Dictation without Notated Signposts

(*Appendix, p. 348*)

The initial pitch or pitches, but not necessarily the initial rhythmic durations, will be given for each of the exercises. Listen to the complete excerpt, particularly to motivic exchanges, before beginning to write. The key and tempo may be established beforehand by agreement, but it is more challenging if this is not done.

108.

109.

Allegretto

110.

Beethoven, Quartet, Op.74, IV, Var.4

Allegretto

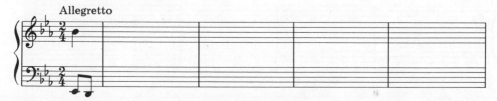

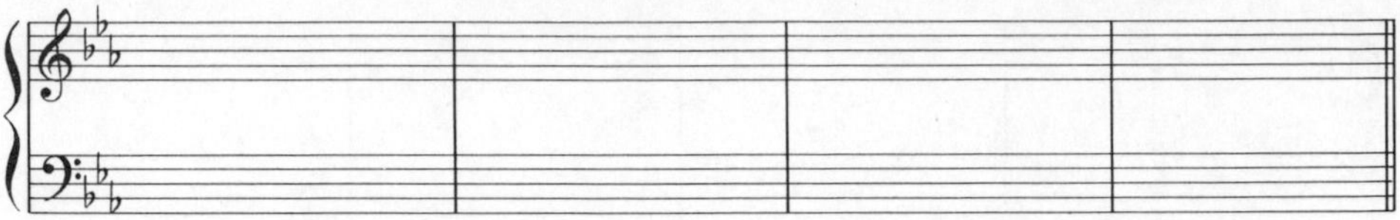

111.

Beethoven, Quartet, Op.18, No.3, II

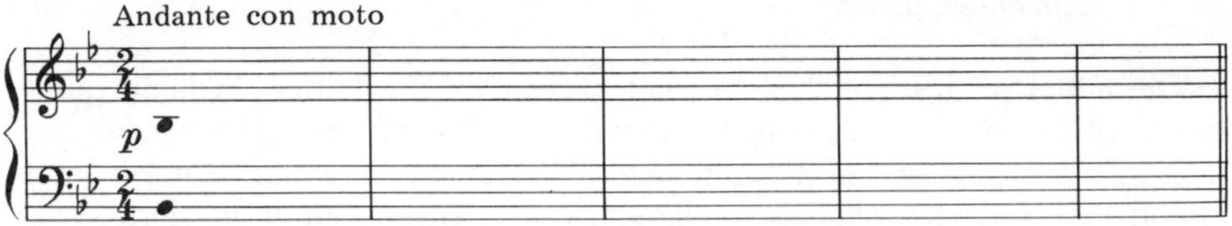

Andante con moto

112.

Mendelssohn, Andante con Variazioni, Op.82, No.10

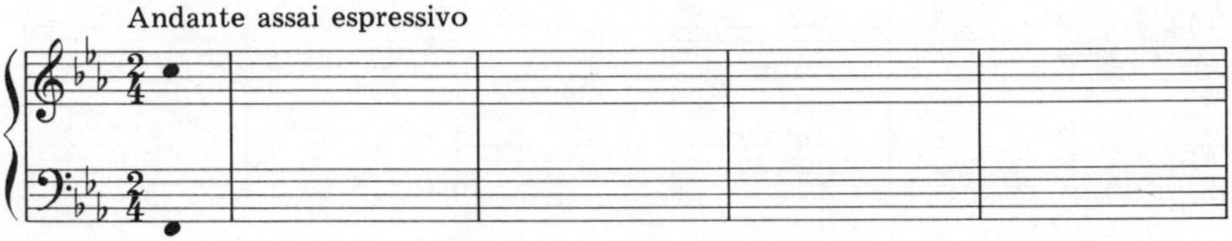

Andante assai espressivo

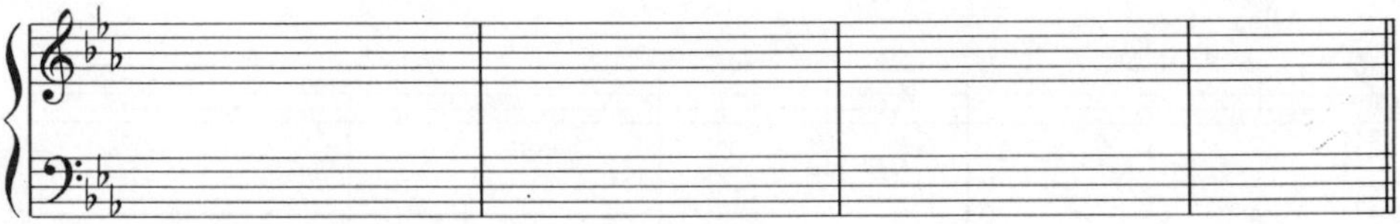

113.

Bach, Trio Sonata, B.M.V.1037, III

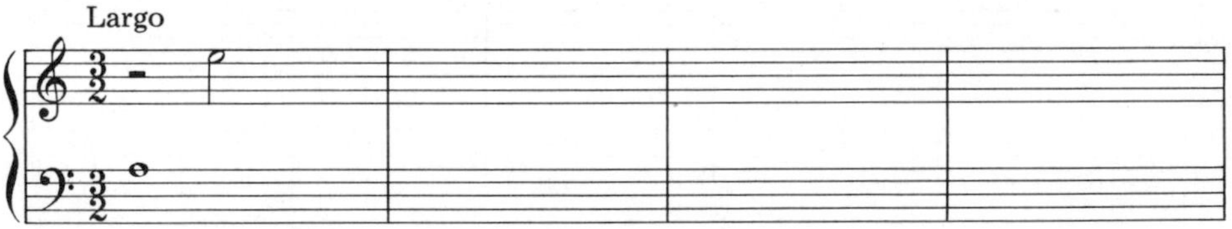

Largo

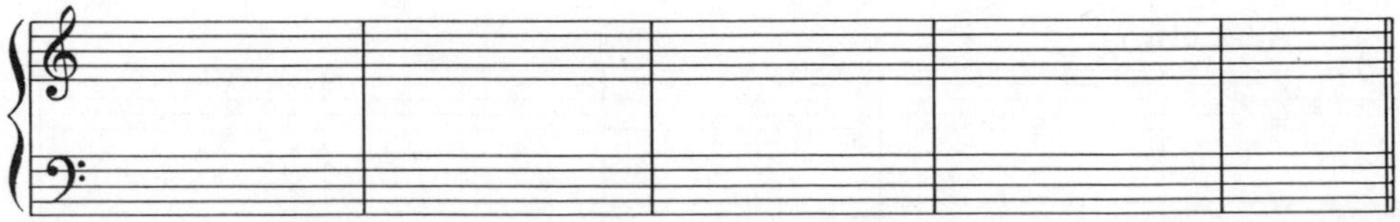

Error Detection

(Appendix, p. 350)

These excerpts from literature will be performed incorrectly, as in previous chapters. Stop the music when you hear an error and correct it immediately, or make a check mark over each passage where an error occurs, later notating the errors directly on the score with a colored pencil. Errors will occur in either the rhythm or the melody, and either singly or in a series. Concentrate on the errors in series first, then on single errors. When an error has been identified and corrected, that segment of the passage should be played correctly thereafter. Neither tempo nor key should be established beforehand.

114.

Brahms, Symphony No.2, I

115.

Bach, Gavotte, French Suite No.4

116.

Brahms, Symphony No.2, I

Allegro non troppo

117.

Bach, Trio Sonata B.M.V.1039, IV

Presto

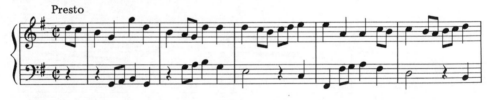

118.

Brahms, Symphony No.2, II

Adagio non troppo (poco grazioso)

Analytical Listening

(Appendix, p. 354)

119–
126.

Discuss each of the following passages in terms of its character, effect, and organization. In other words, describe "what happens" and "how it is accomplished." Consider particularly the interrelationships among the various musical factors that are operating (rhythm, melody, meter, accents, climax areas, sequences, dynamics, texture, register, range, etc.). Make your summaries as cogent as possible.

XXIV

Summary Review: Harmony Analytical Listening

Harmony is aurally more complex, and, as a result, often more frustrating to the student listener than the equally important musical elements of melody, rhythm, and counterpoint. As with the previous chapter, use this review as a diagnostic tool, returning to the appropriate previous chapter for more detailed study when a particular problem is uncovered. Review that chapter methodically and thoroughly, and, as always, resist the temptation to linger over that which seems easiest, while slighting those problems that are vexing. Remember that with persistent practice you can improve, however slowly. If you encounter a stumbling block you cannot surmount, despite intense repeated efforts, abandon that problem for awhile (a couple of weeks, a month, maybe two or three months), but *return to it later*. During the hiatus you may unconsciously be working on the problem, and you may find that when you return to it later some of the problem may have dissolved or even disappeared. You may have to return to the problem again and again before significant progress is made, and your achievement may never match your high expectations or the accomplishment of other musicians you know, but in all likelihood there is some compensating area of musicianship in which you excel to a degree envied by others. Throughout your lifetime, you must continually aspire to be an ever better musician, recognizing your weaknesses and continually striving to improve.

The bulk of this chapter is concerned with harmony at three levels—chord structure, chord function (harmonic progression), and modulation. Generally, in each of these areas there will be a cumulative progression from the simple to the complex. This review chapter will not adhere strictly to the order of the text, where new chords, concepts, and procedures were introduced gradually and progressively. In this chapter, all chords will be considered at the same time, and from the outset, all chords will be employed in the review of harmonic progressions.

CHORD STRUCTURE

Chords are chosen by composers for use in a particular context on two bases primarily—their color (their quality or type) and their function within the particular harmonic progression. The most common chord types are the major and minor triads, both of which are constructed of two unequal thirds, the lower third of which gives the chord its name. Both exhibit a perfect fifth, and hence are relatively stable chords. A diminished triad consists of two minor thirds and hence sounds darker than a minor triad. Its unstable diminished fifth tends to resolve down. If another minor third is added to a diminished triad, a diminished seventh chord results. As with the simpler diminished triad, the diminished intervals tend to resolve inward. If another minor third is added to the diminished seventh chord it will form an enharmonic octave with the root of the chord; in other words, a diminished seventh chord divides an octave into precisely equal parts. As a result, there is no distinguishing interval which will determine the position of the chord and thereby its root, and since any member may function as the root, the chord will normally be heard as being in root position, however it may be spelled.

An augmented triad consists of two major thirds in consecutive order, producing an augmented fifth. Another major third added to an augmented triad produces the enharmonic octave of the lowest chord tone. Thus the augmented triad divides the octave precisely into three equal parts (all major thirds), whereas the diminished seventh chord divides the octave precisely into four equal parts (all minor thirds). The augmented triad, like the diminished seventh chord, does not have an aurally perceivable root.

The V^7 chord occurs almost as frequently as the simpler dominant triad, and is constructed with an additional minor third added to the dominant triad, forming a minor seventh between root and topmost voice.

In summary then, major and minor triads both exhibit a perfect fifth formed of a major and a minor third. Consecutive major thirds produce an augmented triad. Consecutive minor thirds produce either a diminished triad or a diminished seventh chord, depending upon the number of chord members. A V^7 is always a combination of a major triad with a minor seventh.

If the root of the chord is not in the bass, the chord is said to be inverted. With triads, an inversion will produce an interval of a fourth which, if on top when the chord is outlined from the bottom up, indicates a first inversion, and if on the bottom, a second inversion.

The inversion of a seventh chord will produce the characteristic interval of a second, which, if on top, indicates a first inversion, if in the middle, a second inversion, and if on the bottom, a third inversion.

PERFORMING

Chord Outlining

Sing these broken chords on a neutral vowel or use numbers, being always conscious of the chord type (quality, color) and its position (inversion).

Major and Minor

1.

Perform also with *minor* triads.

2.

Also minor.

3.

Also minor.
Diminished

4.

5.

6.

a.

b.

Diminished Seventh

7.

Allegro

8.

Allegretto

Augmented

9.

10.

Dominant Seventh

11.

12.

Broken Chords with Inversions

13. Move the bass upward by half steps for each new set. Perform with triads of all types.

14. Move upward by half steps. Use triads of all types.

15. Move upward by half steps.

16. Move upward by half steps.

Composite Chords

17.

18.

LISTENING

Identification of Chord Type

(Appendix, p. 358)

Identify the following chords by type (major, minor, augmented, diminished, diminished seventh, or V⁷). They may be heard in any position, in any register, and with any spacing. Either name the chord type as each is played, or write it after the appropriate number. There will be a brief silence between chords, since no functional relationship is intended.

19. 1 2 3 4 5 6 7 8 9 10 11 12

20. 1 2 3 4 5 6 7 8 9 10 11 12

Identification of Chord Position

(*Appendix, p. 359*)

Determine the specific position (root position or inversion) of each of these chords as well as the chord type. Both the augmented triad and the diminished seventh chord may be assumed to be in root position. Since no functional relationship is intended between chords, a brief pause will separate chords.

21. 1 2 3 4 5 6 7 8 9 10 11 12 13

22. 1 2 3 4 5 6 7 8 9 10 11 12 13 14 15

Chord Type and Position in Progressions

(*Appendix, p. 360*)

On the first hearing, identify each chord type as it is played; on a second hearing (if necessary) determine the position of each chord. Answers may be verbal, or you may write them below the given bass line.

23.

24.

25.

Dictation

(Appendix, p. 361)

Notate each chord *above* the given bass note. Listen particularly for the chord position and the chord factor in the soprano. Chords will contain either three or four notes.

26.

Notate each chord *below* the given soprano note. Listen particularly for the chord position and the chord factor in the bass. Chords will contain either three or four notes.

27.

Notate each chord either above or below the given pitch, depending upon the direction of the arrow.

28.

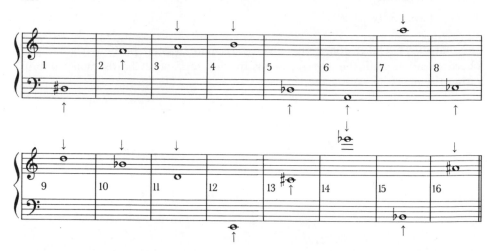

CHORD FUNCTION—HARMONIC PROGRESSION

In tonal music, chords are based on the underlying scale of a particular key and relate to one another in a functional manner. Normally, melodic movement (voice leading) from one chord to another is as smooth as possible, with as little pitch change as possible (unless the *difference* between chords is deliberately emphasized). Obviously those chords that share the most pitches in common will be most like one another and will be considered most closely related, while those having no tones in common will sound most unlike one another.

The most fundamental chord relationship in tonal music is the dominant to tonic progression (V-I). The dominant and tonic may be regarded as polar chords, the dominant containing the single strongest (most pressing, unstable) melodic pitch (the leading tone), and the tonic containing as its root the most fundamental pitch (the most stable, the keystone tonic pitch). Those chords containing the leading tone are usually regarded as dominant-functioning, while the I and vi chords (both containing the tonic) are regarded as tonic-functioning. The IV and ii chords, both containing the fourth scale degree, are the subdominant triads.

In the chart of chord functions (Figure 1, below), the most frequent chord progressions occur from left to right, the primary motion being from the tonic to the dominant and return, with the subdominant functioning as a "way-station" in a predominant capacity, or as an area of momentary contrast to the tonic, to which it immediately returns.

Figure 1: Chord Functions

	Tonic	Subdominant	Dominant	Tonic
Primary Triad:	I	IV	V	I
Secondary Triad:	vi	ii	vii°	vi

iii

Chord movement *within* a functional category is usually *from* the primary *to* the secondary triad, rather than the reverse.

In general, a progression between chords whose roots are a fourth or fifth apart is quite strong, as is a progression in which the root moves *down* by a third. Root movement *up* a third is weaker, and root movement up or down by step connects chords with no pitches in common, creating a progression with maximum contrast between chords.

Just as in language, certain words are frequently found in close juxtaposition, forming a single thought unit (*in the* house, *in the* car, *in the* store), so certain chords occur in conventional patterns to express simple common musical ideas. Neighboring chord patterns, involving motion away from, and immediately back to, a given chord, are particularly common and usually involve a tonic-dominant relationship. Almost all the uses of the $\frac{6}{4}$ chord occur in standard patterns (passing, pedal, and cadential). Other common chord patterns are I-I⁶-IV, I-IV-V-I, ii-V, V²-I⁶, I-iii-IV, and the consecutive first inversion progression. Many other patterns exist and may be practiced as entities along the lines of other pattern exercises in earlier chapters. It is useful to aurally recognize these stock progressions as harmonic clichés, and to perceive them as you would most common prepositional phrases in language—as larger entities with a simple purpose, rather than as unique combinations of words or chords.

Certainly the most common harmonic cadences are recognized as standard patterns when they are used conventionally. The authentic cadence and the half, plagal, and deceptive cadences should be routinely practiced until they can be identified almost without thinking.

Recognizing standard progressions as entities enables the perceptive listener to better appreciate an unusual chord progression or an interesting variant of an anticipated standard pattern.

LISTENING

Determining Chord Roots

(*Appendix, p. 362*)

As a means of preparation for harmonic dictation involving all triads, sing the chord root (not necessarily the bass) of each chord as these progressions are played. Sound the root as soon as possible after the chord has been played; on a subsequent hearing write the chord numeral for each different chord; finally determine the exact position of each chord and write the proper Arabic numbers for the figured bass. The primary object is to recognize true chord changes (not just changes of position or texture) and determine the root of each new chord as quickly as possible. As before, treat the bass of a cadential I $^6_4$ chord as the root. The key will not be established; always assume the initial chord to be the tonic.

29.

30.

31.

32.

Moderato

Determining Cadences

(*Appendix, p. 363*)

33– Sing the chord roots of these cadence progressions and identify each ca-
39.   dence by type (authentic, half, plagal, or deceptive). The key and meter
      should be established before each progression. For additional practice,
      determine also whether the cadence is perfect or imperfect and masculine
      or feminine.

PERFORMING

Linear Chord Changes

As you sing the following exercises, observe the changes of chord function
and the voice leading between chords, particularly the relationship of common
tones.

40.

Allegretto

41.

42.

43.

44.

Four-Voice Chord Progressions

Four individuals or groups of people are needed for the following exercise, each to sing a different part. They will be given the specific spacing of the initial chord and the chord numerals of the progression. Using only the chord

numerals, and without referring to the progression written out in notation,
they are to sing, with proper voice leading and doubling, the desired progression. The tempo should be comfortably slow and even throughout. With
increased skill, the tempo may be accelerated. The voice leading should be
critically observed by all other listeners and corrected as errors occur. Use
letter names, preferably, or a neutral vowel.

Suggested progressions:

45.

g: i V VI iv i$^6_4$ V^7 i

46.

d: i V$^6_5$ i V$^4_3$ i^6 iv V V$^6_5$ i

47.

e: i VI iv ii^{o6}V V$^6_5$ i iv i

48.

F: I IV^6 V^6 I vii^{o6} I^6 ii^6 I$^6_4$ V^7 I

49.

D: I o^7 I vii^{o6}iii IV I$^6_4$V I

50.

c: i o^7 VI^6 V$^6_4$ i^{6}ii^{o6}V7 i

51.

A: I vi I$^6_4$IV I^6 V vi o^{7}I

LISTENING

Error Detection with a Given Chord Series

(Appendix, p. 365)

You are to imagine the sound of each of these chord series, which will be
played incorrectly. On the first hearing, listen to the complete series, noting

where the errors occur. On subsequent hearings, stop the music and correct the errors as they occur. Errors may occur singly or in a series and will increase in frequency and complexity through the course of the exercises.

52. g:　i　iv　V　i　iv⁶　V　i

53. d:　i　V⁶　i　i⁶　iv　iv⁶　i $\frac{6}{4}$　V　i

54. e♭:　i　i⁶　V　V⁶　i　iv　i $\frac{6}{4}$　V⁷　i

55. E♭:　I　vi　V　vi　IV⁶　I $\frac{6}{4}$ ii⁶　V²　I⁶　IV　iii⁶　V⁷　I

56. A:　I　IV⁶　V　V²　iii　ii　o⁷　I　V $\frac{4}{3}$　I⁶　ii⁶　I⁶　IV　o⁷　I

57. Andantino
e: $\frac{3}{8}$ i　i⁶　iv $\Big|$ V $\Big|$ i⁶　iv⁶　V $\Big|$ iv　iv⁶ $\Big|$ V　V⁷ $\Big|$ i $\Big\|$

58. Allegretto
b: $\frac{6}{8}$ i　VI $\Big|$ o⁷ $\Big|$ o⁷　i $\Big|$ V⁷ $\Big|$ iv　V $\Big|$ i $\Big\|$

Error Detection from Score

(Appendix, p. 367)

Each of the following excerpts is correctly notated but will be incorrectly performed. Stop the music when you hear an error, and correct the performer. It is also excellent practice to make a written response to the errors, making a check mark in the score over each error you hear, later notating the incorrect variants directly on the printed score with a colored pencil. The key and tempo should *not* be established before each excerpt is played.

59.

Schumann, "Ein Traum"

60.

Schumann, "Abendlied"

61.

Mozart, *Die Zauberflöte,* Act II—opening

62.

Beethoven, Sonata, Op.13, I

63.

Mozart, *Die Zauberflöte,* Act I

Error Detection from Memory

(*Appendix, p. 371*)

64–   Carefully study each excerpt for a brief period, memorize it, then raise
68.   your hand whenever you hear an error in the performance. Correct it if
       possible, but recognition of an error is still more important than correction
       by memory. After going through each excerpt once, correcting errors, you
       may reexamine the score; all subsequent hearings will follow this reexami-
       nation. Errors will occur in chord type, chord position, or chord function.
       Only harmony—*not* rhythm and melody—is a factor in the incorrect per-
       formances.

64.

65.

66.

67.

68.

Four-Voice Dictation

(*Appendix, p. 373*)

Write the appropriate chord numerals below the bass clef as well as notating the soprano and bass voices. In most of the exercises, certain information will be given to you; in others, you must infer everything yourself. Blanks indicate the number of chord changes in each measure.

The object of these exercises is to correlate the chord function (Roman numerals) with the melodic lines of the soprano and bass. It does not matter whether you concentrate first on the harmonic aspects or the melodic aspects. Eventually you should listen to both aspects simultaneously, since they are equally important, though at any given moment one or the other may predominate. Ultimately you should try to notate the tenor and alto lines also, but the outside lines are far more important in terms of musical flow.

The tonality will be established before each exercise in a new key.

69.

73.

Beethoven, Op.2, No.3, II

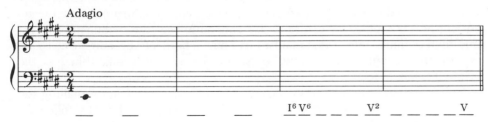

74.

Beethoven, Op.14, No.2, II

75.

Beethoven, Sonata, Op.10, No.1, II

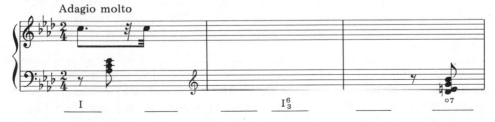

MODULATION

Modulation, the process of harmonic transition from one tonal center to another, may be effected by a variety of means, the most common of which are pivot chord and direct chromatic motion. In pivot chord modulation, a chord common to both keys acts as a "valve," diverting the musical flow from one path to another. Immediately following the pivot chord the harmony clearly proceeds in the new key. Direct chromatic modulation may be accomplished without a pivot chord, by chromatic melodic motion in at least one of the voices into a dominant-functioning chord of the new key. To be an effective modulation, the new key should be as clearly established as the original key had been.

Hearing modulations requires recognition of the foreign tones signalling the new key and relating the new tonal center to the original key. The following exercises explore these factors by a mixture of performing and listening:

1. As the progression is played, sustain the tonic of the original key, shifting to the tonic of the new key after the modulation occurs. *Variant:* Focus on, but do not sing, the tonic of the original key. After the progression is completed, sing the original tonic, then the new tonic. Describe the change of key (e.g., up a major third; C Major to e minor).

2. Raise your hand when you first hear the foreign tones signalling the new key; then determine whether the modulation was accomplished by means of a pivot chord or by direct chromatic modulation. This determination is often difficult, but the presence of stepwise chromaticism in at least one voice usually indicates direct chromatic modulation. After determining the type of modulation, proceed as follows:

Pivot Chord: As the progression is replayed, identify the function of the pivot chord in the original key (e.g., ii⁶). If possible, also determine the key to which the modulation occurred and the function of the pivot chord in the new key (e.g., vi⁶).

Direct Modulation: As the progression is replayed, determine whether the modulation is accomplished through a descending seventh, common tone, leading tone, or a combination of means. Try also to determine in which voice(s) the modulatory motion occurs. Direct chromatic modulation can be very complex. Therefore, don't be discouraged if you cannot hear all the factors operating at any given time. It is more important to recognize *when* it occurs than *how* it occurs, and to hear the relationship between the two tonalities.

3. As the progression is again replayed, write the Roman numerals of the chord progression as it unfolds. It will be useful to preestablish the number of measures in a given progression and to draw the appropriate bar lines on a blank sheet of paper.

4. As the progression, now familiar, is replayed again, write the soprano and bass lines in dictation. If possible, also notate the tenor and alto parts, but the outer voices remain more essential. Use a separate sheet of score paper.

Modulation Exercises

(*Appendix, p. 375*)

76. B♭ $\frac{2}{2}$

77. A♭ $\frac{2}{2}$

78. c   C

79. c $\frac{2}{2}$

80. d $\frac{3}{4}$

81. a $\frac{3}{4}$

82. g $\frac{4}{4}$

Four-Voice Dictation

(*Appendix, p. 378*)

Write the appropriate chord numerals below the bass clef as well as notating the soprano and bass voices. Certain information is occasionally given, especially for unexpected chords. The blanks indicate the number of chord changes in each measure. At least one modulation occurs in each exercise and you should fully indicate the pivot chord (occurring directly before the first chord with functional chromaticism) or, if there is no common chord, the point where the direct modulation occurs (directly on the chord with functional chromaticism, if the previous chord is not common to both keys).

As before, the object of these exercises is to correlate the chord function (Roman numerals) with the melodic lines in the soprano and bass. If possible, divide your attention between the melodic and harmonic aspects, listening to both simultaneously. If this is too difficult, listen to the counterpoint first, later inferring the chords from your melodic observations. At any given moment, either the melodic or the harmonic factor may predominate, and your attention will be guided in such instances. It is excellent practice, as always, to write the alto and tenor lines as well, but the outside lines still predominate. It may be impractical to attempt writing the inner voices in certain styles (melody with moving accompaniment, instrumentally-conceived piano sonata, etc.)

The tonality will be established before each exercise in a new key, and the exercises will be repeated as necessity demands.

83.

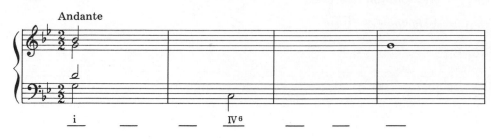

84.

Bach, Chorale, No.7

85.

Bach, Chorale, No.88

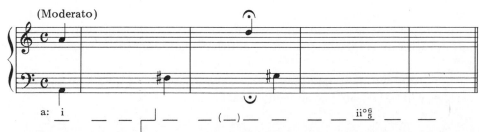

86.

Mendelssohn, *Christus*

E♭:   IV⁶ — — — — — — vii°⁶ — —

— — iii — — — ii⁶₅ — —

87.

— — — — i — ii° — — — —

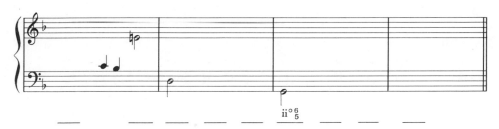

— — — — ii°⁶₅ — — — —

Error Detection with a Given Chord Series

(*Appendix, p. 379*)

You are to imagine the sound of each of these chord series, which will be played incorrectly. On the first hearing, listen to the complete series, noting when the errors occur. On subsequent hearings, stop the music and correct the errors as they occur. Unlike earlier chapters, where the errors occurred singly or occasionally in short series, in these exercises there are some longer series of errors, including modulations through the wrong pivot chord or to the wrong key. Nonharmonic tones sometimes occur as well, depending upon the exercise. The initial exercises are in block chords; later exercises contain more rhythmic variety. The key, but not necessarily the tempo, will be established beforehand.

88.

Moderato

f#: $\frac{2}{2}$ i   V$_4^6$ i^6 V^6 IV^6 V^7 I

A⌐vi^6

89.

Moderato

C: $\frac{2}{2}$ I   V^6 I^6 V$_5^6$ I   V^7 I

E♭

90.

Andante

c#: $\frac{3}{4}$ i   iv | V   i   iv^6 | V$_5^6$ I^6 V | I   ‖

A ⌐vi^6

91.

Allegretto ♩.   ♩   ♪   ♩   ♪ ♩.

B♭: $\frac{6}{8}$ ♪♪♪ | I   ii^6 V | vi   V^6⌐○^{7} | i^6 V | i   ‖

c

92.

Molto moderato ♩   ♩ ♩   ♩ ♩ ♩

E♭: $\frac{4}{4}$ I   iii   vi | ii^6 V   I | ○^{7} i$_4^6$ iv   iv^6 | i$_4^6$ V   i   ‖

g

Error Detection from Score

(Appendix, p. 381)

Each of the following excerpts is correctly notated but will be performed incorrectly. Stop the music when you hear an error, and correct the performer. Allow a reasonable segment to be played before stopping the flow of the music, especially if an error occurs immediately. It is always excellent practice to mark the errors directly on the score, notating them with a colored pencil. Key and tempo should *not* be established before each excerpt is played.

93.

Verdi, *La Traviata,* Act I

94.

Brahms, Variations, Op.9,

95.

Schumann, "Volksliedchen"

96.

Schumann, "An den Sonnenschein"

97.

Beethoven, Piano Concerto No.5, I

Allegro (moderato)

Analytical Listening

(Appendix, p. 385)

98– Discuss each of the following passages in terms of its character, effect,
103. and organization. As before, describe "what happens" and "how it is accomplished." Consider matters of chord choice and usage, harmonic
rhythm, and key changes and relationships in addition to the other musical factors that are operating (rhythm, melody, climax, sequences, dynamics, texture, etc.). Make your summaries brief and precise, and be
sure to include aesthetic as well as technical considerations.

Appendix

Chapter XV

Determining Chord Roots—
Root Position and First Inversion

(*Text, p. 11*)

Play these chords evenly at a moderate tempo. The listener is to sing the root of each chord as it is played. On subsequent hearings he will, if possible, write the chord numerals beneath the bass line.

33.

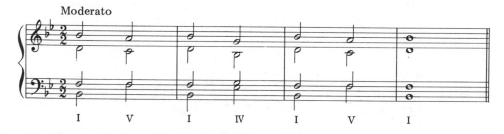

I   V   I   IV   I   V   I

34.

i   V   i   iv^6 V   V^7 i

35.

I ——— 6   V   I^6 IV   V^7 I ———

36.

Reduced from J.S.Bach

$$I \quad I \quad I^6 \quad IV \quad IV^6 \quad I \qquad I \quad V\binom{6}{5}I \quad V \quad I^6 \quad I \quad V \quad {}^7 \quad I$$

37.

Clementi, Op.35, No.3, 3rd mvt.

$$I \qquad V^6 \qquad I \qquad V^6 \qquad I$$

38.

$$i \qquad iv \qquad i \qquad iv \quad V \qquad i \qquad iv$$

$$i^6 \quad iv \quad i^6 \quad V \qquad i \quad V \quad i$$

Recognition of a Specific Progression
(*Text, p. 13*)

Before playing each of the following exercises, announce the chord progression isolated at the beginning of the excerpt. The listener is to raise his hand whenever he hears the specified chord progression. Do not establish the key, tempo, and meter unless absolutely necessary. Repeat the passages for additional practice, isolating different chord progressions (IV-V; I-V⁶, etc.). Find, or invent, other progressions of similar difficulty.

39.
I–IV

40.
i–iv

41.
V⁷–I

Beethoven, Op.49, No.2, 2nd mvt.

42.
V⁷–I

C.M. von Weber, Op.7

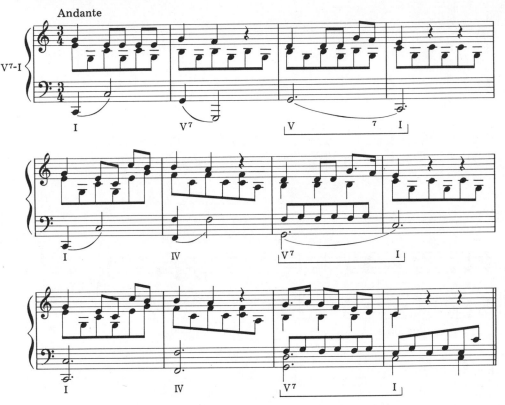

Reuse the exercises above, specifying a different chord progression.

Two-Voice Dictation

(*Text, p. 13*)

The listener is to write the Roman numeral for each implied chord, then the soprano and bass notes, if possible. Establish the tonal center, but preferably not the tempo or meter. If possible, two different instruments should be used for the dictation. Repeat as necessary.

43.

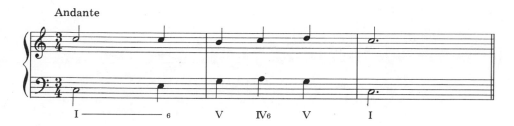

44.

45.

46.

47.

Clementi, Op.36, No.2, 2nd mvt.

I   V₆   I   V₆   I   IV   V   I₆   (I)

Four-Voice Dictation

(Text, p. 15)

The listener is to write the Roman numeral for each chord on the first hearing; on subsequent hearings he will write the bass and soprano voices. He may also write the alto and tenor voices, but this is optional. Establish the tonality before each exercise, except for those marked with an asterisk. For those exercises, the initial soprano and bass pitches are given in the text, and the listener must infer the key center from the context. Play these conservatively slowly.

48.

I   V   I   I   V   I   I   V₇   I   I   V₇   I

49.

i   iv   i   i   iv   i   i   V   i   i   iv   V   i

50.

I   IV₆   V I   V₆ I   V I

51.

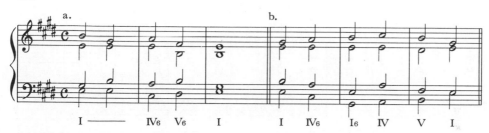

I ——— IV₆ V₆ I   I IV₆ I₆ IV V I

52.

I   V₆   I ——— 6 V ——— 7 I

53. *

i — 6 iv — 6 V — 6 i   iv   i

54. *

I   IV   I   IV₆ V V₇ I V₇ I

Error Detection

(Text, p. 16)

Only the Roman numerals—not the score—are printed in the text. The listener is to raise his hand when he hears any departure from the given series, and, if possible, he should correct the error. Play the excerpts as notated. The circled numerals are the errors under which the correct chord is given. For additional practice, reuse the exercises, inserting other errors.

55.   56.

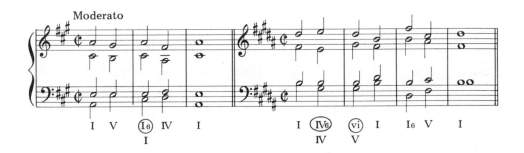

57.

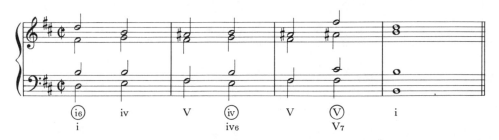

58.

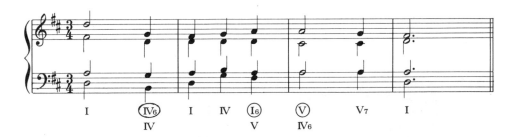

59.

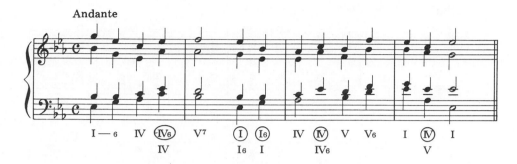

60.

Error Detection from Score

(Text, p. 17)

As the following excerpts from literature are played, the listener will make a check mark over each deviation from the printed score in the text. On subsequent hearings, he will notate the errors directly in the score. Preferably you should *not* establish tempo, meter, or tonality before beginning. As before, play the lower score; the correct differences as given in the text are written in the upper staves.

61.

Schumann, *Freue Dich, O Meine Seele*

Play

62.

Crüger, *Herr ich habe missgehandelt*

Play

63.

Chopin, Mazurka (Op.Post.)

Cantabile

64.

Grieg, *Ase's Death*

Andante doloroso

Error Detection by Memory

(Text, p. 18)

The listener is to carefully study each exercise before it is played. He is to memorize it, then stop the music by raising his hand whenever he detects an error. After each exercise has been played once, he may reexamine the score. All further hearings will be based on this reexamination. If possible, he is to correct each error as it occurs. For additional practice, replay the exercises with different errors. Even better, use a composition with which the class as a whole has come into recent contact or which will be a significant part of their experience in the near future.

65.

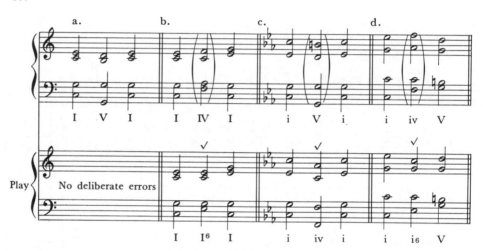

66.

67.

No deliberate errors

68.

Moderato   Andante

Play

69.

Allegretto

Play

70.

Chapter XVI

Two-Voice Rhythmic Dictation

(Text, p. 24)

Use two separate pitch levels for the parts. Initially, establish the tempo before beginning; later this procedure may be dropped. Three hearings should be sufficient; additional hearings should be an exception.

11.

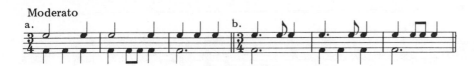

12.

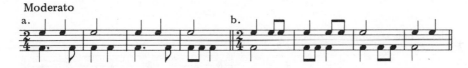

13.

14.

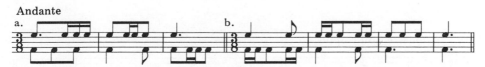

15.

Dictation with Notated Signposts

(*Text, p. 27*)

Use piano, two voices, or two instruments in performing the following exercises. Repeat only as often as necessary commensurate with the listener's ability. To the extent that it is reasonable, play each exercise in its entirety without breaking it into segments or playing each line separately. Establish the key and tempo before beginning each exercise.

22.

23.

24.

25.

26.

Bach, Chorale No.81

(Andante)

27.

Allegro

28.

Tchaikovsky, 6th Symphony, 4th mvt.

Andante (molto)

29.

30.

31.

Dictation without Notated Signposts

(*Text, p. 29*)

The initial pitch (or pitches) is given in the text, but not necessarily the initial rhythmic value. Avoid establishing the tempo and tonic if possible, depending upon the listener's skill. Repeat the exercises as little as possible. If it is necessary to divide the excerpts into smaller fragments, do so in the longest segments possible. No written signposts are provided for the listener; repetition will, no doubt, be necessary.

32.

33.

34.

35.

36.

37.

Franck, Prelude, Chorale and Fugue

38.

Allegro

39.

Bach, Chorale No.68

(Andante)

40.

Flowing

41.

Mendelssohn, "Hope," Op.38, No.4

Andante

42.

Haydn, *The Creation*, No.2

Allegro moderato

Error Detection

(Text, p. 32)

The excerpts printed below are incorrect variants of the excerpts correctly notated in the text. Play (or sing) the excerpts as they are printed below. The fragments printed on the upper staves are the correct version as given in the text.

On the first hearing, listeners will mark the points where errors occur. On subsequent hearings they will notate the errors as they hear them directly on the score, or they may respond orally, stopping and correcting the music as they encounter errors.

Three or four hearings should be sufficient. The listeners' notated errors should be checked against the music printed below as soon as possible after finishing the exercises.

43.

Mendelssohn, "Folk Song," Op.53, No.5

Allegro con fuoco

44.

Brahms, Romance, Op.118, No.5

45.

Bach, Chorale, No.107

46.

Haydn, *The Creation,* No.2

47.

Brahms, *Variations on a Theme of Joseph Haydn,* Var.3

48.

49.

Haydn, *The Creation*, No.29

Adagio (Andante)

50.

Haydn, *The Creation,* No.27

51.

Chopin, "Valse Brilliante"
(Moderato)

52.

Bach, Italian Concerto, III
Allegro (Presto)

53.

Franck, Sonata for Violin and Piano, IV

Chapter XVII

Soprano and Bass Factors

(Text, p. 41)

Play each chord separately, pausing between chords. The listener is to sing the soprano note, then the bass note, then outline and identify the triad quality and position.

10.

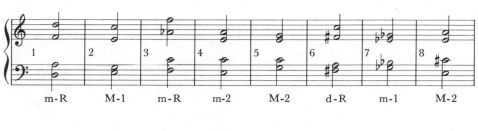

11.

Identification of Chord Progressions in a Series

(Text, p. 43)

The listener is to respond by raising his hand when he hears the specific chord progression announced at the beginning of each exercise. Do not establish key, tempo, or meter unless absolutely necessary. Feel free to invent similar progressions for additional practice.

17.

18.

19.

Allegro moderato

I-IV-I

20.

Moderato molto

i - iv - V
or
iv⁶ - V

21.

Mozart, Sonata, K.283, I

Allegro

V⁶- I

I   IV⁶   I$^6_4$ V⁷   I

Determining Chord Roots—Root Position, First Inversion, and Cadential $^6_4$ Progressions

(*Text, p. 43*)

Play these exercises evenly, possibly emphasizing the bass somewhat. The listener is to sing the *root* of each chord as it is played. He is to regard the bass as the *root* of the $^6_4$ chord, since the resolution of the cadential $^6_4$ is always to V. On subsequent hearings, he is to write the chord numerals below the line given in the text. It is good practice, especially at first, to sing the tonic, subdominant, and dominant scale degrees as a means of orientation within the particular key prior to beginning each exercise.

22.

i   V   i⁶   iv   i$^6_4$ V⁽⁷⁾   i

23.

Mozart, Sonata, K.332, I

I ——————————— (V) I⁶ ——— V ————————— I

(V)   I⁶ ——— V⁽⁷⁾ ——— I   V⁷   I   V⁷   I

24.

Mozart, Sonata, K.280, III

I   (V⁶₅ of IV)   IV ——————— V⁽⁷⁾ ——————— I

25.

Vivaldi, "Domine Deus" from *Gloria*

I ——————— V⁶ ——————— IV⁶ ——————— V

(I⁶₄) ——————— (V) ——————— I ——— V ——— I

26.

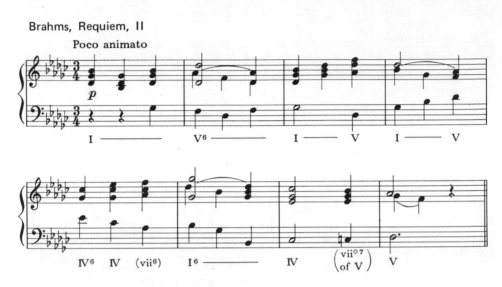

Brahms, Requiem, II
Poco animato

Two-Voice Dictation

(*Text, p. 45*)

The listener is to write the chord numerals below each implied chord and then notate the soprano and bass lines. Establish the tonal center, but preferably not the tempo or meter. Repeat as necessary.

27.

Moderato

28.

Adagio

29.

30.

31.

Vivaldi, "Laudamus Te" *(Gloria)*

Four-Voice Dictation

(*Text, p. 46*)

The listener is to write the Roman numeral for each chord on the first hearing; on subsequent hearings he will write the bass and soprano voices. He may also write the alto and tenor voices, but this is an optional matter. Establish the tonality before each exercise, except for those marked with an asterisk. For those exercises, the initial soprano and bass pitches are given in the text, and the listener is to infer the key center from the context. Play them rather slowly and repeat as necessary.

32.

33.

34.

35.

36.

37.*

Chopin, Mazurka, Op.7, No.1

38.*

Brahms, Op.119, No.4

Error Detection—Chord Series
(*Text, p. 48*)

The score is not printed in the text—only the chord numerals are. The listener is to raise his hand when he hears any departure from the given series, and, if possible, he is to correct the error. Play the excerpts exactly as notated. The circled numerals are the errors, under which the correct chord is given. Reuse the exercises, inserting other errors.

39.

40.

41.

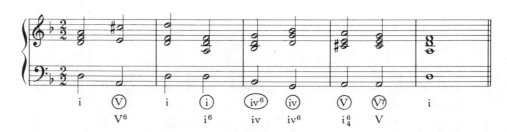

42.

43.

44.

I   (IV IV⁶)   I   IV (IV⁶) (V⁶)   V   I⁶   IV⁶ V (IV) V⁷   (I⁶)
    I⁶ IV   V   IV⁶   I⁶₄   I

Error Detection from Score

(*Text, p. 48*)

As each of the following excerpts is played, the listener is to make a check mark over each departure from the printed score given in the text. On subsequent hearings, he will either notate the errors directly on the score, or stop the music when he hears an error, identifying and correcting it orally. It is better practice if you do not establish tempo, meter, or tonality before listening. Play the lower score; the upper score contains the correct variants as printed in the text.

45.

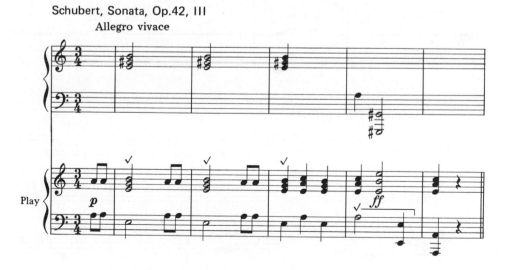

Schubert, Sonata, Op.42, III
Allegro vivace

46.

Vivaldi, Cello Sonata No.3, III

47.

Haydn, Sonata No.43, II

48.

Schumann, Piano Concerto, Op.54, I

49.

Schubert, Sonata in A, II

Andantino

Error Detection by Memory

(Text, p. 50)

The listener is to carefully study each exercise before it is played, memorizing it quickly. Whenever he detects an error, he is to raise his hand to stop the music, and, if possible, to correct the mistake. After an exercise has been played through once completely, he may reexamine the score. All further hearings will be based on that reexamination. For additional practice, replay the exercises with different errors, or select other compositions with which the listener(s) is recently associated and devise errors in them.

50.

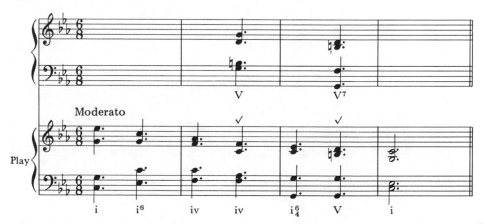

51.

52.

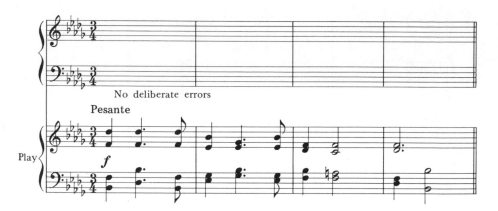

53.

54.

Chapter XVIII

Melodic Dictation

(*Text, p. 58*)

Establish the key and tempo before each exercise. Repeat the exercises as few times as possible. An X over or under certain notes indicates an implied dissonance. Initially you may wish to emphasize these pitches slightly.

Appoggiature

7.

8.

Suspensions

9.

10.

Miscellaneous

11.

12.

13.

14.

Melodic Dictation with a Given Bass

(*Text, p. 60*)

Do not establish the key or tempo beforehand. Repeat each exercise as few times as possible, and divide the longer exercises into shorter segments if necessary. One or more of the lines are given, and the listener is to complete the remainder.

15.

16.

Allegretto

17.

Bach

(Andante)

18.

Mozart, Sonata, K.333, I

Allegro

19.

Mozart, Sonata, K.332, I

Allegro

20.

Bach

(Andante)

Motivic Error Detection

(*Text, p. 65*)

The exercises printed below are incorrect versions of those printed in the text. The correct variants appear in the upper staff. The listener is to interrupt the music when he hears an error and correct it. After an error has been identified and corrected, repeat the passage correctly and continue playing until stopped by the listener. Repeat the process.

23.

Alla marcia

Play

24.

No deliberate errors

Allegro non troppo

Play

25.

Allegretto

Play

26.

Allegro marcato

Play

27.

No deliberate errors

Vivace

Play

28.

29.

Mozart, Sonata, K.284, III

30.

Mozart, Sonata, K.284, III

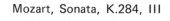

31.

Mozart, Sonata, K.332, III

Allegro assai

No deliberate errors

32.

Brahms, Intermezzo, Op.119, No.2

Andantino grazioso

33.

Brahms, Rhapsody, Op.79, No.2

Molto passionato, ma non troppo allegro

Play

Play

34.

Brahms, Intermezzo, Op.117, No.3

Andante con moto

Play

Dictation with Notated Signposts

(*Text, p. 68*)

Use piano, two voices, or two other instruments. Repeat only as often as necessary, commensurate with the dictation skills of the listener. Long passages may be broken into shorter segments if necessary. It is better aural practice if tempo and key are not established beforehand.

35.

Allegro

36.

37.

38.

Des Prez, "Pleni Sunt Coeli" *(Missa L'Homme Armé)*

39.

Brahms, Symphony No.2, I

Dictation without Notated Signposts

(*Text, p. 70*)

The initial pitch (or pitches) is given, but not necessarily the initial rhythmic value. Tempo and key may be established beforehand, but it is preferable to avoid this practice whenever possible. Repeat as few times as possible, preferably the entire excerpt rather than shorter segments. Repetition will prove necessary since there are no written signposts in the text.

40.

41.

42.

43.

44.

45.

Haydn, "The Lord is Great" *(The Creation)*

Error Detection

(Text, p. 71)

Play the complete incorrect version of each exercise (lower staves); correct passages, as they appear in the text, are on the upper staves.

The listener will either stop the music when he hears an error, making a correction, or he will make a check mark over each error, later notating it. If done orally, repeat each passage with the identified errors played correctly, until all errors have been detected and corrected. Don't be concerned if you should make accidental errors. These should be detected by the listener and corrected along with the printed errors. If the listener notates the errors, it may be necessary to repeat a passage three or four times. The notated errors should always be checked against the music printed below as soon as possible after the exercises are completed. Do not establish key or tempo beforehand.

46.

Bach, Two-part Inventions, I

(Poco allegro)

47.

Haydn, ''Achieved is the Glorious Word'' *(The Creation)*

Vivace (Allegro)

48.

Bach, Fugue 1, *The Well-Tempered Clavier,* I

(Poco adagio)

Play

49.

D. Scarlatti, Sonata in A minor (Kirkpatrick No.3)

(Allegro moderato)

Play

50.

Beethoven, String Quartet, Op.131, I

Adagio, ma non troppo e molto espressivo

51.

Adapted from Corelli, Trio Sonata, II

Presto (Allegro)

52.

Bach, Two-part Inventions, VI

(Allegretto)

No deliberate errors

Chapter XIX

Identification of Dominant Seventh Inversions

(*Text, p. 78*)

Establish the tonality before each of the following exercises. The listener is to identify the specific inversion (or inversions) of the V^7 used in each passage.

9.

10.

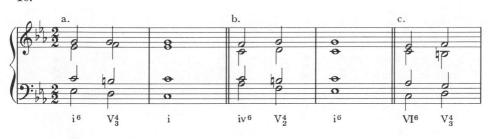

Before playing each of the following passages, specify a particular progression involving an inversion of the V⁷. The listener is to raise his hand whenever he hears the progression. As an alternate procedure, he is to identify each inversion of the V⁷ whenever one occurs.

11.

12.

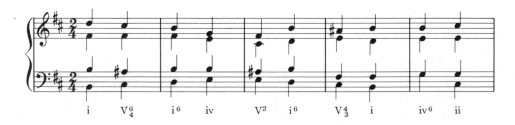

$$V_3^4 \quad i^6 \qquad iv \quad V \qquad VI \quad VI^6 \qquad V_5^6 \quad i \qquad V_5^6 \qquad i$$

Chord Identification

(Text, p. 85)

Before playing each of the following passages, specify a single chord or progression. The listener is to raise his hand when he hears the specified harmony. It is more difficult, and therefore better practice, if the tonality is not established before the exercises.

22.

$$I \quad I^6 \qquad IV \quad ii \qquad I^6 \quad V^7 \qquad I$$

23.

a.

$$i \quad V \qquad iv^6 \quad ii^{o6} \qquad i_4^6 \quad V_2^4 \qquad i^6 \quad V_4^6 \qquad i$$

b.

$$i \quad VI^6 \qquad V_5^6 \quad i \qquad iv^6 \quad VII \qquad III \quad iv \qquad ii^o \quad V^7 \qquad i$$

24.

I   vi   IV   V — 6   I   ii   V   vi   V$^6_5$ vi^6 ii^6 V   I

25.

i   V   i   iv^6 ii^{o6} V   III$^+$ iv^6 iv   i$^6_4$ V$^6_5$ i

26.

i iv V^7 VI ii^{o6} V   i^6 V$^6_4$ i   iv^6 V   VI^6 III iv   i$^6_4$ V^7 i

Identification of a Specified Chord Pattern

(*Text, p. 92*)

Before playing each of the following progressions, announce a specific chord pattern or progression. The listener is to raise his hand whenever he hears the progression. Do not establish the tonality or meter before the exercises. Reuse the exercises with other specified chord patterns, and invent similar progressions for additional practice.

36.

Mozart, Sonata, K.332, 1st mvt.

ii—V

I   I$^6_4$ V   I   — $^6_4$ V

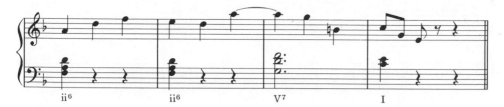

ii⁶   ii⁶   V⁷   I

37.

Mendelssohn, *Christus*

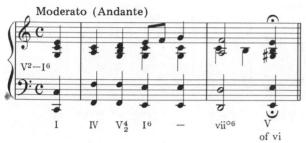

Moderato (Andante)

V²–I⁶

I   IV   V$^4_2$ I⁶   —   vii°⁶   V
of vi

38.

Mozart, Sonata, K.332, 3rd mvt.

Allegro assai

Consecutive
First Inversions

i⁶   VII⁶   VI⁶   v⁶   iv⁶   A⁶   i$^6_4$ V

39.

Mendelssohn, *Christus*

Allegro moderato

Passing$^6_4$, or
V²–I⁶

V⁶   I   V   I   IV⁶   I$^6_4$ V$^4_2$ I⁶

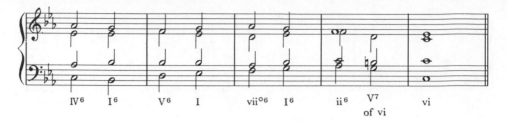

40.

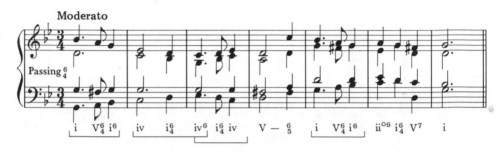

41.

Mozart, Sonata, K.333, 3rd mvt.

Determining Chord Roots

(*Text, p. 92*)

Play these exercises as evenly as possible, emphasizing the bass somewhat at first. The listener is to sing the *root* of each chord immediately after he hears it, and on subsequent hearings to write the specific chord numerals. It is good practice, especially initially, to sing the tonic, subdominant, and dominant scale degrees before beginning, but do not establish the tonality at the piano before beginning.

42.

I   ii   I⁶ IV   ii   V⁷   I

43.

I   V⁶₄   I⁶ IV   ii   V⁷   vi   ii⁶   I⁶₄   V⁷   I

44.

Bach, Chorale: *Von Gott will ich nicht lassen,* No.191

IV⁶   IV⁷   IV   IV²   vii°⁶ °⁷   iii   V⁶₅   I   ii⁶   i⁶₄   V   I

C|I⁷   of iii   a|iv⁶

Four-Voice Dictation

(Text, p. 93)

The listener is to write the chord numerals in the following progressions as well as to notate the soprano and bass voices. Establish the tonality before each exercise in a new key. Play them somewhat slowly at first; err conservatively for the present in matters of tempo.

45.

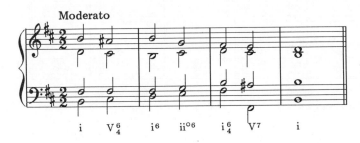

i   V⁶₄   i⁶   ii°⁶   i⁶₄   V⁷   i

46.

i   V⁶   i   iv   i⁶   VI   III   iv   III⁺⁶   VI   ii°⁶ V⁷   i

47.

Beethoven, Op.14, No.2, 2nd mvt.

I   V⁴₃   I⁶   V⁶   I   ii⁶   V   I⁶   V⁴₃   I   V⁴₃   vi   IV   V

                                                                  of vi

48.

Bach, Chorale, No.257

I   vi   iii   IV   V$_2^4$ I^6 ii$_5^6$ V   I   I

F: $\boxed{-6}$ $\boxed{IV^6}$ V^6 I   I^6 V$_3^4$ I

49.

Beethoven, Op.2, No.3, 2nd mvt.

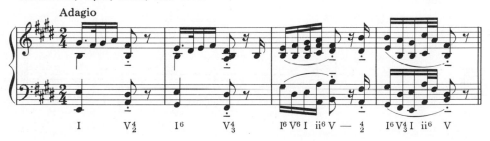

I   V$_2^4$ I^6 V$_3^4$ I^{6}V^{6}I ii^{6}V — $_2^4$ I^{6}V$_3^4$I ii^6 V

50.

Beethoven, Sonata, Op.2, No.2, 2nd mvt.

I   I^6 V$_2^4$ I^6 V$_5^6$ I   V

Error Detection

(*Text, p. 95*)

The score is not printed in the text—only the chord numerals are. The listener is to raise his hand when he hears any departure from the given series, and, if possible, he is to correct the error. Play the excerpts exactly as notated. The circled numerals are the errors, under which the correct chord numeral is given. Reuse the exercises, inventing other errors. Establish the tonality, but not necessarily the tempo, before each exercise.

51.

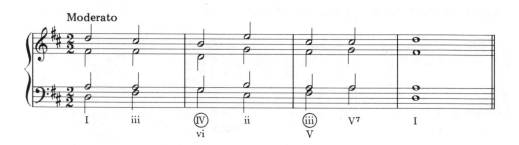

52.

53.

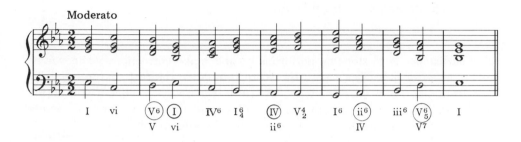

54.

55.

Error Detection from Score

(*Text, p. 96*)

The listener is to stop the performance and make corrections whenever he hears an error at variance with the score printed in the text. If preferred, he might notate the errors directly on his score. It is better practice if you do *not* establish the tempo, meter, or tonality. Play only the lower score; the upper score contains the points of variance as correctly notated in the text.

56.

Mozart, Sonata, K.333, 3rd mvt.

57.

Schubert, *Death and the Maiden,* 2nd mvt.

g: III   III   iv   ii°⁶   V

VI   i⁶₄   iv   B♭⌐vi⁶   °⁷   V   iii⁶   V⁷   I
               i⁶   of V

58.

Beethoven, Sonata, Op.2, No.3, 1st mvt.

59.

Mozart, Sonata, K.283, 1st mvt.

60.

Brahms, Romance, Op.118, No.5

Error Detection by Memory

(Text, p. 98)

The listener is to carefully study each excerpt before it is played, memorizing it quickly. Whenever he detects an error, he is to stop the performance, and, if possible, correct the mistake. After going through each exercise once completely, he may reexamine the score. All further hearings will be based on that reexamination. For additional practice, replay the exercises with different errors, or select other compositions which the listener(s) has recently studied, and devise errors in them.

61.

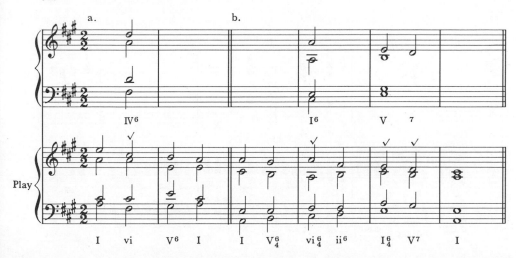

62.

63.

64.

Chapter XX

Two-Voice Rhythmic Dictation

(Text, p. 104)

Play these exercises on two different pitch levels or on two different instruments. You may wish to establish the tempo before each exercise, but this practice should be abandoned whenever possible. Normally, three hearings should be sufficient. If an error is made on the first playing, keep it throughout all subsequent playings. The proper number of bar lines is given in the text.

10.

11.

12.

13.

14.

Motivic Development

(*Text, p. 105*)

Play the basic motive twice before each exercise; then play the entire excerpt. The listener is to describe the techniques of motivic development employed in each excerpt. Normally one hearing should suffice, but a second hearing may be necessary.

15.

16.

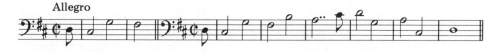

17.

Franck, Symphony in D Minor, I

18.

Mozart, Symphony No.40, K.550, I

* Some theorists would hold that the entire first two measures constitute the motive, and that the first three notes are a germinal "figure." The passage may be analyzed from either point of view, since both views must take into account the developmental procedures employed.

19.

Beethoven, Symphony No.5, I

20.

Brahms, Rhapsody, Op.79, No.1

21.

Brahms, Intermezzo, Op.117, No.3

22.

Brahms, Rhapsody, Op.79, No.2

Dictation with Notated Signposts

(*Text, p. 107*)

Repeat only as often as necessary, according to the listeners' skills. Long passages may be broken into shorter segments if necessary.

25.

26.

27.

Mendelssohn, *Christus*

28.

29.

Bach, "Qui Tollis" (B Minor Mass)

Dictation without Notated Signposts

(*Text, p. 108*)

The initial pitches, but not necessarily the initial rhythm, are given for each exercise. Establish tempo and key beforehand only if absolutely necessary, and repeat as few times as possible.

30.

31.

32.

33.

34.

Mendelssohn, *Christus*

35.

Mendelssohn, *Christus*

Error Detection

(*Text, p. 110*)

Play the entire incorrect version of each exercise (lower staves—correct passages, as they appear in the text, are on the upper staves).

The listener will either stop the music when he hears an error, making an immediate correction, or he will make a check mark over each error, later notating it. If done orally, once an error has been identified and corrected, replay the passage as it should be performed until all errors have been detected and corrected. Don't be concerned if you should make accidental errors. These should be detected and corrected along with the printed errors. If the listener notates the errors, it may be necessary to repeat a passage three or four times. All notated errors should be checked against the music printed below as soon as possible after the exercises are completed. Do not establish tempo or key beforehand.

36.

37.

38.

Brahms, Requiem, II

Allegro, ma non troppo

Play

39.

Bach, Fugue No.2, *The Well-Tempered Clavier*, I

40.

Bach, "Gloria in Excelsis" (B Minor Mass)

41.

Franck, Violin Sonata, IV

42.

Lassus, Motet: *Justus Cor Suum Tradet*

(Gently flowing)

Play

No deliberate errors

Play

Chapter XXI

Identification of a Diminished Seventh Chord
in a Chord Progression
(Text, p. 116)

On the first hearing, the listener is to identify each diminished seventh chord he hears by raising his hand; on the second hearing, he is to name the diatonic chord to which each resolves. Preferably, neither key nor tempo should be established beforehand.

10.

11.

12.

Pivot Chord Exercises

(Text, p. 119)

The following exercises are unlike any thus far encountered. The listener is to respond in one of several ways as follows:

1. As the progression is played, sustain the tonic of the original key, shifting to the tonic of the new key after the modulation occurs. *Variant:* Focus on, but do not sing, the tonic of the original key. After the progression is completed, sing the original tonic, then the new tonic. Describe the change of key (e.g., up a major third; C Major to e minor).

2. As the progression is replayed, raise your hand when you hear the foreign tone(s) in the chord immediately following the pivot. As the progression is replayed again, identify the function of the pivot chord in the original key (e.g., I^6). If possible, also determine the key to which the modulation occurred and the function of the pivot chord in the new key (e.g., VI^6).

3. As the progression is again replayed, write the Roman numerals of the chord progression as it unfolds. It will be useful to preestablish the number of measures in a given progression and to draw the appropriate bar lines on a blank sheet of paper.

4. As the progression, now familiar, is replayed again, write the soprano and bass lines in dictation. If possible, also notate the tenor and alto parts, but the outer voices remain more essential. Use a separate sheet of score paper.

As a general practice, in all these exercises the key should be established beforehand and a moderate (considerate) tempo employed.

13.

14.

15.

16.

17.

18.

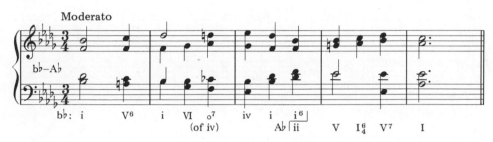

19.

20.

Exercises with Direct Chromatic Modulation

(Text, p. 120)

Follow the four procedures described above, modifying the second procedure as follows: the listener is to raise his hand when he hears the direct modulation occur. As the exercise is replayed, he is to identify the voice in which the chromatic motion occurs, and the function of the chord immediately preceding the chromatic leading tone.

21.

22.

23.

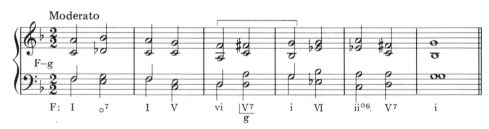

24.

25.

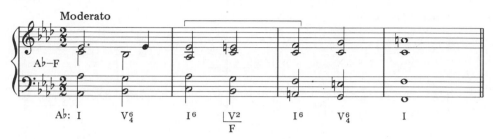

26.

27.

More Exercises with Direct Chromatic Modulation

(*Text, p. 122*)

Follow the standard four procedures. In procedure 2, the listener is to determine whether the modulation is effected through a descending seventh, common tone, leading tone, or a combination of means, and, if possible, in which voices the modulatory motion occurs. Be sure to establish the original key before beginning.

28.

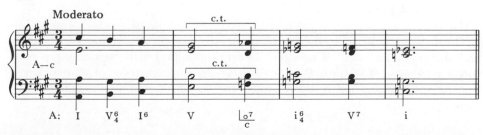

29.

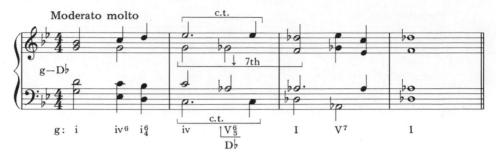

30.

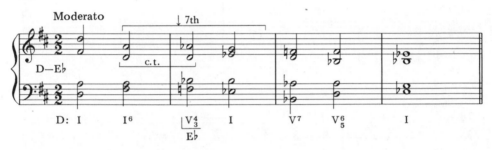

31.

More Four-Voice Dictation

(*Text, p. 122*)

The listener is to write the chord numerals as well as soprano and bass—also the tenor and alto, if possible. Multiple playings will be necessary according to need. Establish the tonality before each exercise in a new key. Regard the tempi conservatively, since the exercises will prove difficult to many.

32.

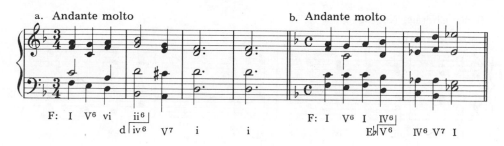

33.

34.

Mendelssohn, *Christus*

35.

Bach, Chorale, No.160

36.

Kuhlau, Sonatina, Op.20, No.3, II

37.

Error Detection with a Given Chord Series

(Text, p. 125)

As in earlier chapters, only the chord numerals—*not* the score—are printed in the text. The listener is to raise his hand when he hears any departure from the given series (after the first hearing), and, if possible, he is to correct each error. Play the excerpts exactly as notated. The circled numerals are the errors, under which the correct chord numerals are given. Reuse the exercises, inventing other errors. Establish the key, but not necessarily the tempo, before each exercise.

38.

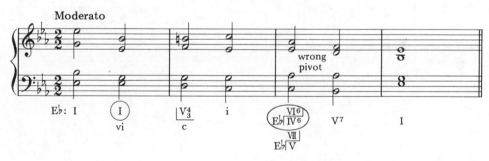

39.

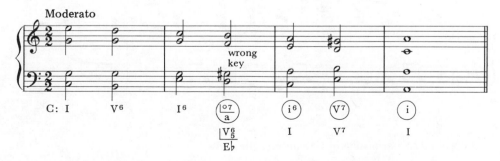

40.

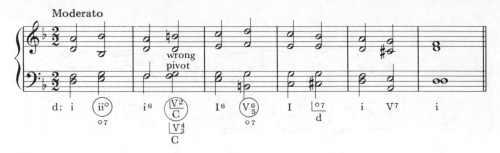

41.

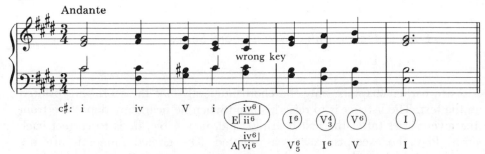

42.

Mendelssohn, *Christus*

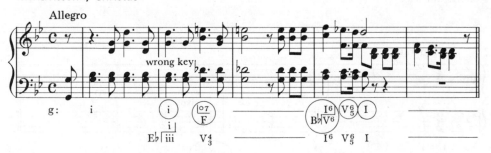

43.

Klengel, Concertino for Cello and Piano, II

Reprinted by permission of G. Schirmer, Inc.

312

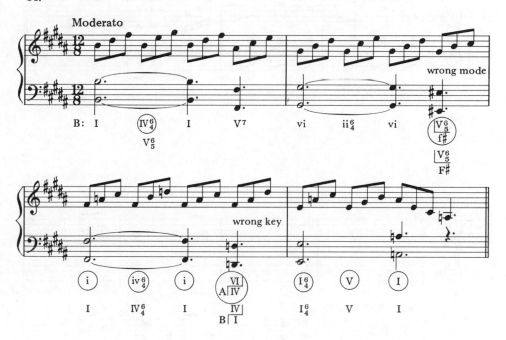

Error Detection from Score

(*Text, p. 126*)

The listener is to stop the performance and make corrections whenever he hears an error at variance with the score printed in the text; or, if preferred, he might notate the variants directly in his score. Do *not* establish the key or tempo beforehand. As before, play only the lower score; the upper score contains the points of variance as notated correctly in the text. Inadvertent errors are certainly as valid as contrived errors, so don't be too concerned if you make errors you had not intended; however, some practice is recommended beforehand, since some of the errors run counter to one's musical expectations.

45.

Kuhlau, Sonatina, Op.55, No.2, II

46.

Chopin, Mazurka, Op.68, No.3

47.

Bach, Sarabande (French Suite, I)

48.

Beethoven, Sonata, Op.49, No.1, I

49.

Mozart, Sonata, K.280, I

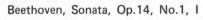

50.

Beethoven, Sonata, Op.14, No.1, I

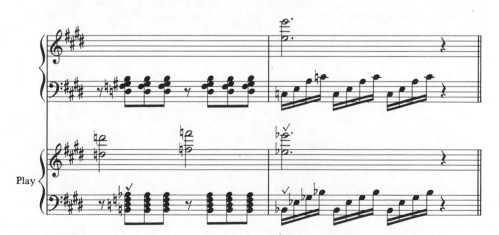

51.

Beethoven, Sonata, Op.13, I

Chapter XXII

Recognition of Irregular Divisions

(Text, p. 134)

The listener is to raise his hand when he recognizes an irregular division of the beat. On subsequent hearings he is to identify the nature of each irregularity and be prepared to notate them. Do not establish either key or tempo beforehand.

15.

16.

17.

18.

19.

Beethoven, Sonata, Op.13, 2nd mvt.

Adagio cantabile

20.

Tchaikovsky, Symphony No.6, 3rd mvt.

Allegro molto vivace

21.

Fauré, "Après un Rêve"

Andantino

22.

Schumann, Piano Sonata, Op.22, No.2, 2nd mvt.

Andantino

Error Detection—Syncopation, Hemiola, Irregular Divisions

(Text, p. 140)

As with previous exercises of this nature, the listener is to make a check mark over (or under) the errors he detects; on subsequent hearings he is to stop the music and correct each error, or series of errors, when it occurs. Perform the passage correctly once an error has been identified and corrected. Use two different pitches for the contrapuntal lines.

Perform the continuously notated lines. These are the incorrect versions of which the correct variants are shown above or below the line. You need not establish the tempo, since it is indicated in the text.

A word of advice. It is helpful to practice the exercises before presenting them, since some passages are too intricate to sight-read as usual. If you encounter problems performing them, proceed directly to the second half of the procedure, and have the listeners correct the errors immediately. Inadvertent errors are every bit as valid as deliberate errors.

45.

Allegro non troppo

46.

Vivace (in one)

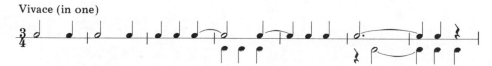

47.

Adagio

48.

Moderato

No deliberate errors

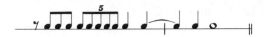

49.

Adagio

50.

Allegro

51.

Tempo di Valse

Error Detection in a Melodic Context

(Text, p. 143)

As in previous chapters, the listener is to stop the music and correct an error whenever one occurs. The score is given in the text, so you should not establish key or tempo beforehand, unless absolutely necessary. The passages are incorrect as notated; the correct variants occur on the extra staff. A little preparatory practice works wonders, as always. A few passages are sufficiently difficult that no suggested errors are given. They may just occur naturally.

52.

Beethoven, Sonata, Op.2, No.2, 1st mvt.

53.

Haydn, Symphony No.92 (Oxford), 1st mvt.

54.

Beethoven, Sonata Op.2, No.1

55.

56.

Brahms, Cello Sonata, Op.38, 3rd mvt.

Analytical Listening

(*Text, p. 145*)

The listener is to describe the organization of each melody after the passage has been played, particularly with regard to the important musical elements being utilized, either singly or in combination. Several of these require a fairly skilled pianist, but a little practice is of value to everyone. If the passages are too difficult, substitute others or play a recording, cautioning the listener to carefully delineate the melodic line from the other elements.

58.

Beethoven, Sonata, Op.7, I

59.

Schumann, Sonata No.2, Op.22, I

60.

Beethoven Sonata, Op.10, No.1, Finale

61.

Mozart, Serenade, K.525, "Eine Kleine Nachtmusik"

62.

Brahms, *Variations on a Theme by Haydn,* Var.VII

Grazioso

BROADER ASPECTS OF RHYTHM

Analytical Listening

(*Text, p. 148*)

These passages are to be described as in the exercises above, with the emphasis on large patterns created by the relationship between rhythm and melody.

63.

Beethoven, Sonata, Op.2, No.3, 1st mvt.

Allegro vivace

64.

Beethoven, Sonata, Op.2, No.3, 1st mvt.

Allegro con brio

65.

Brahms, Rhapsody, Op.79, No.1

66.

Chopin, Prelude, Op.28, No.6

67.

Bach, French Suite No.1, Sarabande

68.

Brahms, Rhapsody, Op.79, No.2

Instrumentally-Conceived Counterpoint
—Error Detection

(Text, p. 149)

Some of these exercises are "bears" and require a fair degree of skill. As before, however, any error is valid, whether preplanned or not. After an error has been identified and corrected, that segment should be played correctly thereafter. Neither key nor tempo should be established beforehand. A few passages are correctly notated, so no variants are shown above. If you can play these passages without problems—wonderful!

69.

70.

Bach, Invention XIV

(Andante con moto)

71.

Mozart, Symphony No.41, "Jupiter," K.551, 4th mvt.

72.

Bach, Invention VI

Chapter XXIII

RHYTHM

Recognition of Specified Factors

(Text, p. 159)

The listener is to raise his hand when he hears the rhythmic pattern specified (the figure before each exercise). If he makes an error, perform that
segment slowly, after which he should slowly intone the passage with the
correct pattern. Intone the exercises or perform them on an instrument. You
need not establish the tempo beforehand, since it is given in the text.

24.

25.

26.

27.

Allegro moderato

28.

Marcato

29.

Moderato

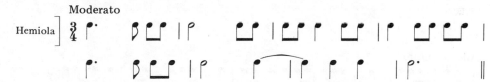

Dictation

(*Text, p. 161*)

Follow standard procedures. All two-voice dictation should be performed at two different pitches or on two different vowels. As always, the less repetition, the more challenging the exercise.

38.

Andante

§ ♪♪♪ | ♩ ♪♩ ♪ | ♪♪♪ ♩. ‖

39.

Allegretto

⅔ ♩ | ♩. ♩ | ♩ ♩ ♩♪ | ♩ ♩ | ♩ ♩ ‖

40.

Allegro

C ♪. ♪ | ♩ ♩ ♩♩ | ♩ ♩♩ | ♩♩ ♪♩ ‖

41.

Poco adagio

42.

Andante con moto

43.

Grazioso

44.

Allegro molto

45.

Moderato

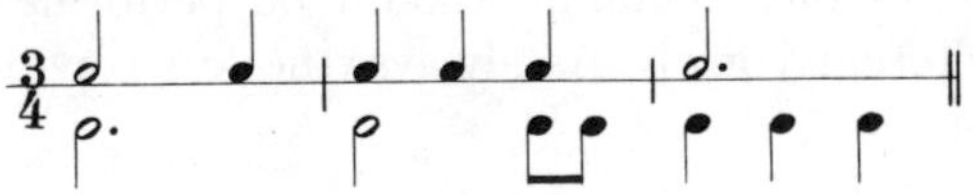

46.

Moderato

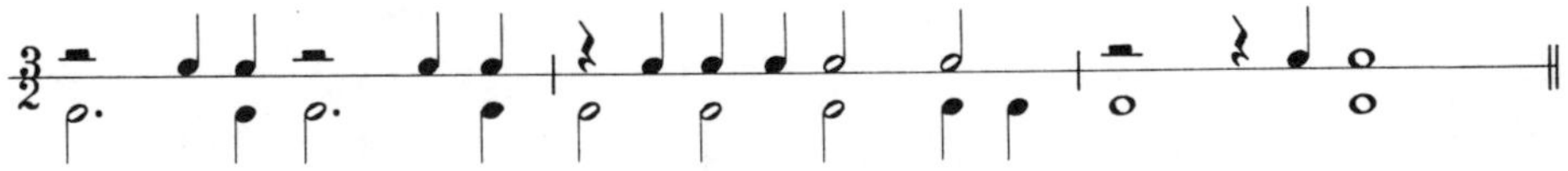

47.

Alla marcia

48.

Moderato

Error Detection

(*Text, p. 163*)

Intone or play the following exercises, which are incorrect variants of the passage as printed in the text (the correct patterns are shown in parentheses above or below the passage). Initially you may establish the tempo beforehand; later this should be eliminated. Use two different pitches, instruments, or vowels for the two-voice passages, and do not repeat the passages too frequently.

49.

Allegretto

50.

Andante

51.

Allegro moderato

52.

Poco andante

53.

Allegro

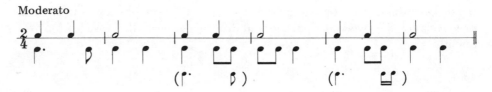

54.

Moderato

55.

Grazioso

56.

Poco adagio

57.

Allegro non troppo

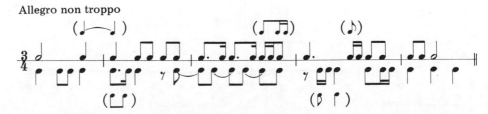

58.

Poco allegro

No deliberate errors

MELODY

Error Detection

(Text, p. 168)

The melodies printed below are incorrect versions of those printed in the text. The correct variants appear in the upper staff. The listener is to interrupt the music when he hears an error and make corrections after the initial hearing. Always perform that segment of the passage correctly after an error has been identified and corrected. Repeat the passage until all errors have been identified and corrected.

69.

Mendelssohn, "Lost Happiness," Op.38, No.2

Allegro non troppo

Play

Play

Play

70.

Brahms, Intermezzo, Op.118, No.2

71.

Mendelssohn, "The Return," Op.85, No.5

72.

Beethoven, Sonata, Op.14, No.2, I

Play

Play

73.

Beethoven, Sonata, Op.22, IV

Play

Play

74.

Franck, Sonata for Violin and Piano, I

Allegretto ben moderato

75.

Chopin, Ballade No. 1, Op. 23

Dictation with Guideposts

(*Text, p. 170*)

The listener is given several notated clues to assist in transcribing these exercises. The exercises should not be repeated too frequently. In some instances a complete bass line is given, over which the listener is to write the melody.

76.

Clementi, Sonatina, Op.36, No.4, II

77.

Clementi, Sonatina, Op.36, No.2, III

78.

Mendelssohn, The Wanderer, Op.30, No.4

79.

Mendelssohn, Contemplation, Op.36, No.1

80.

Schumann, Piano Concerto, Op.54, III

Dictation without Guideposts

(*Text, p. 172*)

Establish key and meter, if desired, but hold repetition to a minimum. Longer passages may need to be broken into shorter segments.

81.

82.

83.

84.

85.

86.

87.

Mendelssohn, "Consolation," Op.30, No.3

88.

Bach, Fugue No.2, *The Well-Tempered Clavier,* I

89.

Mendelssohn, "Funeral March," Op.62, No.3

90.

Mendelssohn, "Folk Song," Op.53, No.5

COUNTERPOINT

Dictation with Notated Signposts

(*Text, p. 176*)

Use piano, two voices, or two instruments, as before. Repeat only as often as necessary, but longer passages may need to be broken into shorter segments. It is better practice if tempo and key are not established beforehand.

101.

102.

103.

104.

Beethoven, Quartet, Op.59, No.I, II

105.

Mendelssohn, Fugue, Op.35

106.

Beethoven, Quartet, Op.18, No.2, IV

107.

Beethoven, Quartet, Op.59, No.3, II

Dictation without Notated Signposts

(*Text, p. 179*)

The initial pitch (or pitches) is given, but not necessarily the initial rhythmic durations. Key and tempo may be established beforehand, especially at first, and repetition should be kept to a minimum, as always. It *will* be necessary to repeat, however, and longer passages may be divided into more manageable segments.

108.

109.

Allegretto

110.

Beethoven, Quartet, Op.74, IV, Var.4

Allegretto

111.

Beethoven, Quartet, Op.18, No.3, II

Andante con moto

112.

Mendelssohn, Andante con Variazioni, Op.82, No.10

Andante assai espressivo

113.

Bach, Trio Sonata, B.M.V. 1037, III

Largo

Error Detection

(Text, p. 181)

Play the complete incorrect versions of each exercise (lower staves); correct passages, as notated in the text, are on the upper staves. Do not establish key or tempo beforehand.

The listener will stop the music when he detects an error and will suggest an immediate correction. Once corrected, play that segment correctly thereafter. Inadvertent errors are equally as valid as deliberate errors. Continue the process until all errors have been identified. If the listener notates the errors rather than responding orally, several hearings may be necessary. The notated errors should always be checked against the music printed below as soon as possible after the exercise is completed.

Certain of the passages are technically challenging and should be practiced beforehand.

114.

Brahms, Symphony No.2, I

115.

Bach, Gavotte, French Suite No.4

116.

Brahms, Symphony No.2, I

117.

Bach, Trio Sonata B.M.V. 1039, IV

118.

Brahms, Symphony No.2, II

Analytical Listening

(*Text, p. 183*)

The listener is to describe the character, effect, and organization of each passage after it has been played, with particular emphasis on the interrelationships among the various musical elements operating to produce the musical flow.

Advance practice is encouraged, since a few excerpts may prove technically challenging. You may wish to substitute a recording, or use other works of literature, the organization of which are readily perceptible aurally.

119.

Brahms, Symphony No.2, I

120.

Beethoven, Symphony No.3, II

121.

Beethoven, Symphony No.3, II

Compare 121 with 120, the former a variant of the latter.

122.

Beethoven, Symphony No.3, I

123.

Brahms, Symphony No.2, IV

124.

Dvořák, Quartet, Op.51

125.

Mozart, Sonata K.284, III, Var.IX

126.

Beethoven, Sonata, Op.13, III

Allegro (tranquillo)

Chapter XXIV

Identification of Chord Type

(*Text, p. 189*)

Separate each chord from the surrounding chords, since no progression is intended. The listener will either name the chord type or will write it in the text.

19.

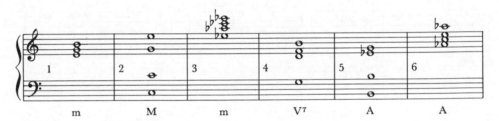

20.

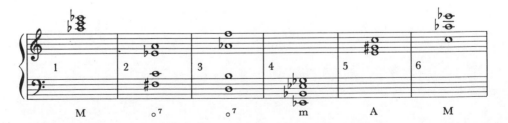

7	8	9	10	11	12
d	m	A	Dom.7th	d	∘7

Identification of Chord Position

(Text, p. 190)

Separate the chords as before. The listener is to determine the specific position of each chord, assuming the augmented triad and the diminished seventh chord always to be in root position.

21.

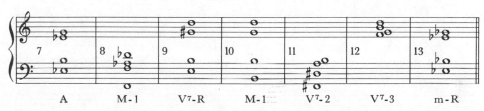

1	2	3	4	5	6
M-R	m-1	M-2	∘7	m-2	d-1

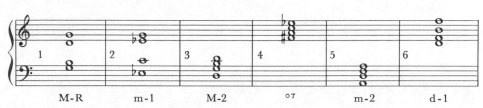

7	8	9	10	11	12	13
A	M-1	V7-R	M-1	V7-2	V7-3	m-R

22.

1	2	3	4	5	6	7
M-1	A	V7-2	d-R	∘7	m-R	M-1

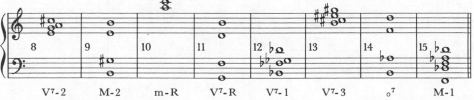

8	9	10	11	12	13	14	15
V7-2	M-2	m-R	V7-R	V7-1	V7-3	∘7	M-1

359

Chord Type and Position in Progressions

(*Text, p. 190*)

Establish the key of each exercise before it is played. The listener is to determine the chord types on the first hearing, and the specific position on the second hearing.

23.

m-R   m-1   d-1   M-R   M-R M-1   d-R   m-1   M-1   m-R

24.

M-R   V⁷-3   M-1   M-R   m-R   V⁷-2   m-1   M-R   V⁷- 3   M-1

V⁷-1   M-R   V⁷-R   M-1   m-1   V⁷-3   M-1   V⁷-2   M-R

25.

m-R   m-R   m-2   m-1   o⁷   M-R   M-1   V⁷-R   M-R

Dictation

(Text, p. 191)

The bass note is given in the text, and the listener is to notate the chord *above* it. Separate the chords.

26.

The soprano note is given in the text, and the listener is to notate the chord *below* it. Separate the chords.

27.

Either bass or soprano is given, and an arrow indicates whether to notate the chord above or below the given note.

28.

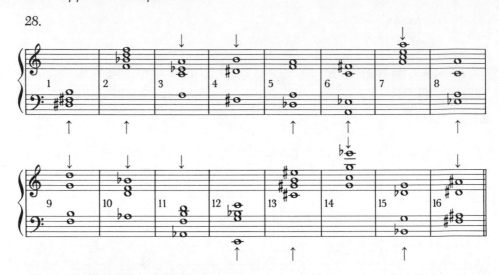

Determining Chord Roots

(*Text, p. 194*)

Play these exercises as evenly as possible, emphasizing the bass somewhat at first. The listener is to sing the *root* of each chord immediately after he hears it, and on subsequent hearings he is to write the specific chord numerals. It is good practice, especially initially, to sing the tonic, subdominant and dominant scale degrees before beginning, but do not establish the tonality at the piano before beginning.

29.

30.

i   iv   i⁶ iv i⁶ V   i   V   i

31.

Andante

I   V⁶₄   I⁶ IV   ii   V⁷   vi   ii⁶   I⁶₄   V⁷   I

32.

Moderato

b: i   V⁶₃   VI⁶ iv⁶│V   vi   V   I   o⁷   ii   vi⁶₄ ii⁶│   V⁷ i⁶₄ V   i
             D │ii⁶   b │iv⁶

Determining Cadences

(*Text, p. 195*)

Establish the key and meter before each progression. The listener is to sing the chord roots of the cadence progressions and identify each by type.

33.

a. Authentic   b. Half

D: I   ii⁶ i   I⁶₄   V   I   d: i   V⁶₄   i⁶   ii°   V

34.

c#:   i   i⁶ iv iv⁶   i⁶ V VI

35.

G: I   I⁶ vii°⁶ I   V   b♭:   i V⁶₅ i   V⁶₄ i⁶ iv   i

36.

D: I   °⁷ vi °⁷ V   I
            of vi   of V

37.

Beethoven, Op.49, No.1

g: i⁶   V⁶₅   i   ii°⁶   i⁶₄   V

38.

Brahms, Romance, Op.118, No.5

F : I V(iii⁶) vi iii (I⁶) IV I

39.

Beethoven, Sonata, Op.7, II

C : IV V⁶₅ V o⁷ vi V⁶₅ I⁶₄ V⁷ o⁷
 of V of vi of V of ii

Error Detection with a Given Chord Series

(*Text, p. 197*)

The score is not printed in the text—only the chord numerals are. The listener is to raise his hand when he hears any departure from the given series, and, if possible, he is to correct the error. Play the excerpts exactly as notated. The circled numerals are the errors, under which the correct chord is given. Reuse the exercises, inserting other errors.

52.

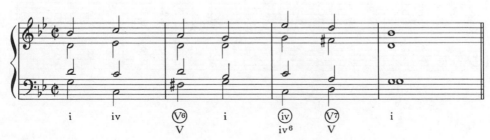

i iv Ⓥ⁶ i Ⓘⓥ Ⓥ⁷ i
 V iv⁶ V

53.

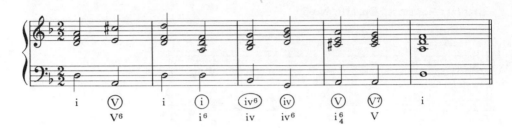

i   Ⓥ   i   i   ⓘⱽ⁶   ⓘⱽ   Ⓥ   Ⓥ⁷   i
   V⁶   i⁶   iv   iv⁶   i⁶₄   V

54.

i   ⓘⱽ⁶   V   V⁶   ⓘ⁶   Ⓥ   i⁶₄   Ⓥ⁶   i
   i⁶   i   iv   V⁷

55.

Moderato

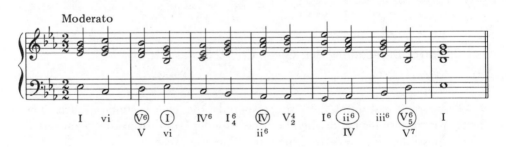

I   vi   Ⓥ⁶   Ⓘ   IV⁶   I⁶₄   Ⓘⱽ   V⁴₂   I⁶   ⓘⁱ⁶   iii⁶   Ⓥ⁶₅   I
      V   vi   ii⁶   IV   V⁷

56.

I   ⓥⁱ   Ⓥ⁷   V²   ⓥⁱ⁶₄   ii   ⁰⁷   I   ⁰⁷   I⁶   Ⓥ²   I⁶   ⓘⁱ   Ⓥ⁷   I
   IV⁶   V   iii   V⁴₃   ii⁶   IV   ⁰⁷

57.

i — 6 (V) (iv) (iv⁶) i⁶ iv⁶ V (iv⁶) (iv) V — 7 i
iv   V —   iv — 6

58.

b :   i (iv) o⁷ —— (V₇) i (o⁷) —— (ii°) V i
    VI   o⁷   V⁷   iv

Error Detection from Score

(Text, p. 198)

The listener is to stop the performance and make corrections whenever he hears an error at variance with the score printed in the text. If preferred, he might notate the errors directly on his score. It is better practice if you do *not* establish the tempo, meter, or tonality. Play only the lower score; the upper score contains the points of variance as correctly notated in the text.

59.

Schumann, "Ein Traum"

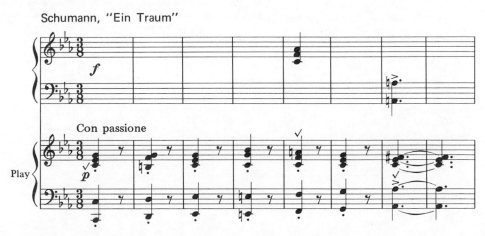

60.

Schumann, "Abendlied"

61.

Mozart, *Die Zauberflöte*, Act II, opening

62.

Beethoven, Sonata, Op.13, I

63.

Mozart, *Die Zauberflöte,* Act I

No deliberate errors

Error Detection from Memory

(*Text, p. 200*)

The listener is to carefully study each excerpt before it is played, memorizing it quickly. Whenever he detects an error, he is to stop the performance, and, if possible, correct the mistake. After going through each exercise once completely, he may reexamine the score. All further hearings will be based on that reexamination. For additional practice, replay the exercises with different errors, or select other compositions which the listener(s) has recently studied, and devise errors in them.

64.

65.

66.

67.

68.

No deliberate errors
Andante

Play

Four-Voice Dictation

(Text, p. 201)

The listener is to write the chord numerals in the following progressions as well as to notate the soprano and bass voices. Establish the tonality before each exercise in a new key. Play the exercises somewhat slowly at first; err conservatively for the present in matters of tempo.

69.

a.

I ——— IV⁶ V⁶ I

b.

I   V   IV⁶ IV   V—— 7   I

70.

i　　V　　i ——— 6　　iv⁶　　V ——— 7　　i

71.

i　iv　iv⁶　V　i⁶　i　iv⁶　i　V⁶　i

72.

i　V⁶　i　iv　i⁶　VI　III　iv　III⁺⁶　VI　ii°⁶　V⁷　i

73.

Beethoven, Op. 2, No. 3, 2nd mvt.

I　V⁴₂　I⁶　V⁴₃　I⁶V⁶ I ii⁶V ——— ⁴₂　I⁶V⁴₃ I ii⁶ V

74.

Beethoven, Op.14, No.2, 2nd mvt.

75.

Beethoven, Sonata, Op.10, No.1, II

Modulation Exercises

(*Text, p. 205*)

The listener is to respond in several different ways, according to the following instructions:

1. As the progression is played, sustain the tonic of the original key, shifting to the tonic of the new key after the modulation occurs. *Variant:* Focus on, but do not sing, the tonic of the original key. After the progression is completed, sing the original tonic, then the new tonic. Describe the change of key (e.g., up a major third; C Major to e minor).

2. Raise your hand when you first hear the foreign tones signalling the new key; then determine whether the modulation was accomplished by means of a pivot chord or by direct chromatic modulation. This determination is often difficult, but the presence of stepwise chromaticism in at least one voice usually indicates direct chromatic modulation. After determining the type of modulation, proceed as follows:

Pivot Chord: As the progression is replayed, identify the function of the pivot chord in the original key (e.g., ii⁶). If possible, also determine the key to which the modulation occurred and the function of the pivot chord in the new key (e.g., vi⁶).

Direct Modulation: As the progression is replayed, determine whether the modulation is accomplished through a descending seventh, common tone, leading tone, or a combination of means. Try also to determine in which voice(s) the modulatory motion occurs. Direct chromatic modulation can be very complex. Therefore, don't be discouraged if you cannot hear all the factors operating at any given time. It is more important to recognize *when* it occurs than *how* it occurs, and to hear the relationship between the two tonalities.

3. As the progression is again replayed, write the Roman numerals of the chord progression as it unfolds. It will be useful to preestablish the number of measures in a given progression and to draw the appropriate bar lines on a blank sheet of paper.

4. As the progression, now familiar, is replayed again, write the soprano and bass lines in dictation. If possible, also notate the tenor and alto parts, but the outer voices remain more essential. Use a separate sheet of score paper.

76.

77.

78.

79.

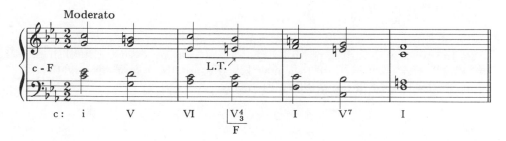

80.

81.

82.

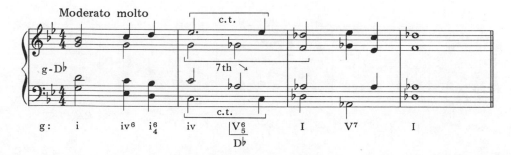

Four-Voice Dictation

(*Text, p. 205*)

The listener is to write the chord numerals as well as soprano and bass—also, the tenor and alto, if possible. Play as often as necessary. Establish the tonality before each exercise in a new key. Regard the tempi conservatively, since the exercises will prove difficult to many.

83.

84.

Bach, Chorale No.7

85.

Bach, Chorale No.88

86.

Mendelssohn, *Christus*

87.

Error Detection with a Given Chord Series

(*Text, p. 207*)

As in earlier chapters, the score is not printed in the text—only the chord numerals are. The listener is to raise his hand when he hears any departure from the given series (after the first hearing), and, if possible, he is to correct the error. Play the excerpts exactly as notated. The circled numerals are the errors, under which the correct chord numeral is given. Reuse the exercises, inventing other errors. Eestablish the key, but not necessarily the tempo, before each exercise.

88.

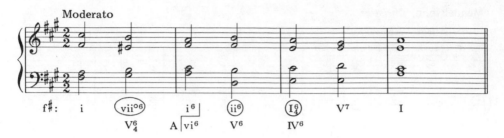

89.

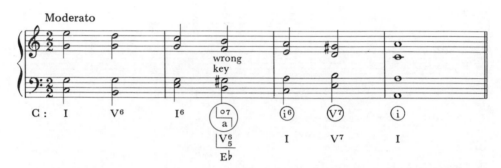

90.

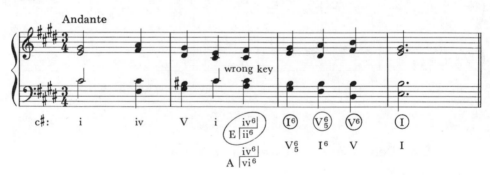

91.

92.

Eb: I   iii   vi   V⁶₅ I   V   ₒ⁷   i   VI   iv   i⁶₄ V   i
                 Bb ii ii⁶ V   I   g   i⁶₄ iv iv⁶
                 vi

Error Detection from Score

(*Text, p. 208*)

The listener is to stop the performance and make corrections whenever he hears an error at variance with the score printed in the text; or, if preferred, he might notate the variants directly in his score. Do *not* establish the key or tempo beforehand. As before, play only the lower score; the upper score contains the points of variance as notated correctly in the text. Inadvertent errors are certainly as valid as contrived errors, so don't be too concerned if you make errors you had not intended; however, some practice is recommended beforehand, since some of the errors run counter to one's musical expectations.

93.

Verdi, *La Traviata,* Act I

94.

Brahms, Variations, Op.9

95.

Schumann, *Volksliedchen*

96.

Schumann, "An den Sonnenschein"

97.

Beethoven, Piano Concerto No.5, I

Analytical Listening

(Text, p. 211)

The listener is to describe the character, effect, and organization of each passage after it has been played, with particular emphasis on the interrelationships among the various musical elements operating to produce the musical flow.

Advance practice is encouraged, since a few excerpts may prove technically challenging. You may wish to substitute a recording or use other works of literature, the organization of which are readily perceptible aurally.

98.

Verdi, *La Traviata,* Act I

99.

Beethoven, Symphony No.1, II

Andante cantabile con moto

100.

Brahms, Sonata, Op.5, II

Andante molto

101.

Beethoven, Sonata, Op.13, I

102.

Mozart, Sonata, K.330, II

103.

Chopin, Prelude, Op.28, No.6